Susan W. Reddin

MONSTER HUNTER
WILDS

GAME GUIDE

Master weapons, Tactics, Hidden Secrets, Legendary Adventures in the Wild, and Endgame Challenge

CHAPTER 1: INTRODUCTION TO MONSTER HUNTER WILDS

1.1 GAME OVERVIEW

Monster Hunter Wilds is the latest installment in Capcom's critically acclaimed *Monster Hunter* series, taking the franchise to new heights with its expansive open-world design, dynamic ecosystems, and immersive combat mechanics. Set in a vast, untamed wilderness teeming with life, this game challenges players to step into the role of a hunter, tasked with tracking and defeating some of the fiercest creatures ever encountered in the series.

Unlike its predecessors, *Monster Hunter Wilds* introduces an interconnected open world with seamless transitions between diverse biomes, from arid deserts and dense jungles to icy tundras and volcanic landscapes. Each environment is not just a backdrop but a living, breathing part of the gameplay, where weather changes, time of day, and ecological interactions directly influence both the hunter and the hunted.

At its core, the game remains true to the series' signature gameplay loop: **track, hunt, and craft.** Players embark on quests to hunt down colossal monsters, harvest their materials, and forge increasingly powerful weapons and armor to tackle even greater threats. However, *Monster Hunter Wilds* amplifies this loop with deeper role-playing elements, improved AI for both monsters and companions, and a more fluid combat system that rewards strategy, preparation, and skill.

Whether you're a veteran of the series or a newcomer drawn to the thrill of the hunt, *Monster Hunter Wilds* offers an experience rich with challenge, discovery, and triumph. This guide will provide you with all the tools, strategies, and insights needed to master every aspect of the game, from basic survival tips to advanced hunting techniques.

1.2 NEW FEATURES AND CHANGES IN MONSTER HUNTER WILDS

Monster Hunter Wilds introduces a wealth of new features and gameplay improvements that elevate the hunting experience to unprecedented levels. Capcom has refined core mechanics while adding fresh elements to keep both veterans and newcomers engaged. Here's a detailed look at the standout features and changes that define this latest installment.

Seamless Open-World Exploration

One of the most significant changes in *Monster Hunter Wilds* is the transition to a fully open-world environment. Unlike previous games, where maps were divided into distinct zones separated by loading screens, this game offers a seamless world with no interruptions. Players can travel across vast, interconnected regions without encountering load times, creating a more immersive and fluid exploration experience.

The environments are dynamic and alive, with ecosystems that react to your actions. Predators hunt prey, weather patterns shift unexpectedly, and natural disasters like sandstorms or avalanches can occur, influencing both exploration and combat.

Dynamic Weather and Day-Night Cycles

The introduction of a dynamic weather system adds a new layer of depth to both exploration and combat. Weather changes aren't just visual they directly affect gameplay. For example:

- **Rainstorms** can make certain monsters more aggressive or alter their attack patterns.
- **Extreme heat** in desert biomes may drain stamina faster unless you're properly equipped.
- **Nighttime hunts** could reveal nocturnal monsters that behave differently than during the day.

Hunters must adapt their strategies based on these environmental changes, making each hunt feel unique and unpredictable.

Enhanced Monster AI and Ecosystem Interactions

Monsters in *Monster Hunter Wilds* are smarter and more reactive than ever. They exhibit realistic behaviors, such as stalking prey, engaging in territorial disputes, or retreating when injured. Monsters can even ambush hunters if they sense weakness, adding an element of surprise to every encounter.

Additionally, ecosystem interactions play a larger role. You might lure a large predator into a fight with another monster to gain an advantage or trigger an environmental hazard to deal massive damage. Understanding these dynamics can turn the tide of difficult hunts.

New Movement Mechanics and Mounts

To help players navigate the expansive world, *Monster Hunter Wilds* introduces new movement mechanics, including the ability to climb more freely, swing across gaps using grappling tools, and even swim in certain areas.

The game also features rideable creatures that act as mounts. These aren't just for fast travel they can assist in combat, help track monsters, or carry additional supplies. Some mounts even have unique abilities that allow you to access otherwise unreachable areas, expanding the scope of exploration.

Revamped Crafting and Gear Customization

The crafting system has been overhauled to offer more flexibility and depth. Players can now:

- **Customize weapons and armor** with modular parts, allowing for tailored builds.
- **Experiment with new crafting materials** that grant special buffs or elemental effects.
- **Upgrade gear on the fly** at field camps without returning to base, streamlining the hunting loop.

These changes encourage experimentation, enabling hunters to adapt their equipment to specific monsters or situations.

Improved Co-op and Multiplayer Integration

Multiplayer has always been a cornerstone of the *Monster Hunter* series, and *Wilds* enhances this with seamless drop-in/drop-out co-op functionality. Whether you're playing solo or with friends, transitioning between single-player and multiplayer feels natural.

The game also introduces **cross-platform play**, allowing players from different consoles and PCs to hunt together. Additionally, new co-op mechanics, like synchronized attacks and combo moves, add depth to team-based strategies.

1.3 TIPS FOR BEGINNERS

Starting out in *Monster Hunter Wilds* can feel overwhelming, especially with its expansive open world, complex systems, and challenging monsters. However, with the right approach and mindset, you'll find yourself thriving in no time. Here are essential tips to help beginners get a strong start on their hunting journey.

Understand the Core Gameplay Loop: Hunt, Gather, Craft

At its heart, *Monster Hunter Wilds* revolves around a simple yet addictive loop:

1. **Hunt Monsters**: Track down and defeat creatures to gather materials.
2. **Gather Resources**: Collect herbs, ores, bones, and other items from the environment.
3. **Craft Gear**: Use the materials you've gathered to forge stronger weapons and armor, allowing you to tackle tougher monsters.

Embrace this cycle early on. Every hunt, even if it feels small, contributes to your overall progress. Don't rush take time to explore, gather resources, and familiarize yourself with different monsters.

Choose the Right Weapon for Your Playstyle

Monster Hunter Wilds features a wide variety of weapons, each with its own unique mechanics, combos, and strategies. Some weapons are fast and agile, while others are heavy and deal massive damage. As a beginner, consider the following:

- **Sword & Shield:** Great for newcomers due to its balance of offense and defense.
- **Long Sword:** Offers fluid combos and good reach without being overly complex.

- **Bow:** Perfect if you prefer ranged combat with quick mobility.

Don't be afraid to experiment with different weapons during training missions. Find one that feels comfortable, but keep in mind that mastering a weapon's intricacies takes time.

Pay Attention to Monster Behavior

Instead of blindly attacking, observe your target's behavior. Monsters have distinct patterns, tells, and weaknesses that you can exploit. Key things to watch for:

- **Movement Patterns:** Is the monster aggressive or defensive? Does it favor certain attacks?
- **Weak Spots:** Most monsters have vulnerable areas, like heads, tails, or wings.
- **Enraged States:** When a monster gets angry, its attack speed and damage often increase. Be extra cautious during these phases.

Patience is your greatest weapon. Study your foe, strike when the time is right, and always be ready to dodge or reposition.

Master Dodging and Stamina Management

Survival in *Monster Hunter Wilds* isn't just about dealing damage it's about avoiding it. Rolling, evading, and managing your stamina bar are crucial for staying alive. Here are some quick tips:

- **Dodge with Purpose:** Don't spam the dodge button. Learn the invincibility frames (i-frames) where your character can pass through attacks unharmed.
- **Watch Your Stamina:** Running, dodging, and certain weapon attacks consume stamina. If it runs out, you'll be vulnerable. Always leave some stamina for emergency evasions.
- **Positioning is Key:** Sometimes, sidestepping or walking out of range is safer than rolling. Stay calm, and don't panic when under pressure.

Don't Ignore the Environment

The world of *Monster Hunter Wilds* is more than just a backdrop it's a tool you can use to your advantage. Look out for:

- **Environmental Traps:** Rocks that can be knocked down, vines that entangle monsters, or ledges for powerful jumping attacks.
- **Flora and Fauna:** Collect plants for healing items, insects for buffs, or small creatures that distract large monsters.
- **Elemental Hazards:** Lava pools, quicksand, and icy terrain can hurt both you and the monsters. Use them strategically.

Prepare Before Every Hunt

Preparation is the difference between success and failure. Before heading out:

- **Eat a Meal:** Meals provide temporary stat boosts like increased health, stamina, or attack power. Always eat before a tough hunt.
- **Check Your Equipment:** Make sure your weapons are sharp, your armor is upgraded, and your inventory is stocked with potions, traps, and other essentials.
- **Review the Monster's Weaknesses:** Knowing whether a monster is weak to fire, ice, or another element can help you choose the right gear.

Don't Fear Failure Learn from It

You will faint. You will fail quests. It's part of the learning process. Every defeat teaches you something new about the game's mechanics, monster behavior, or your own strategies. Instead of getting frustrated:

- Analyze what went wrong.
- Adjust your equipment or approach.
- Try again with a fresh perspective.

The satisfaction of finally overcoming a tough monster after multiple attempts is one of the most rewarding feelings in *Monster Hunter Wilds*.

Take Advantage of Multiplayer

If a hunt feels too difficult solo, don't hesitate to join forces with other players. Multiplayer not only makes hunts easier but also teaches you new strategies by observing how others fight. Communication is key work together, support your team, and share the thrill of victory.

1.4 UNDERSTANDING THE HUNTER'S ROLE

In *Monster Hunter Wilds*, you step into the role of a hunter an elite warrior tasked with tracking, studying, and defeating the world's most formidable creatures. But being a hunter is about more than just wielding massive weapons and slaying monsters. It's about understanding your environment, adapting to different situations, and becoming part of a larger ecosystem. This section will break down what it truly means to be a hunter and how you can fulfill your role effectively.

The Hunter's Purpose: More Than Just Slaying

While the core gameplay revolves around hunting monsters, your role as a hunter extends beyond combat. You're an explorer, researcher, protector, and strategist all in one. The Guild assigns you various quests not just to eliminate threats, but also to maintain balance within the ecosystem.

Your responsibilities include:

- **Tracking Monsters:** Learning their habits, movements, and weaknesses.
- **Studying the Ecosystem:** Understanding how monsters interact with each other and their environments.
- **Gathering Resources:** Collecting materials not just from monsters but also from plants, minerals, and wildlife.
- **Supporting the Community:** Helping settlements thrive by eliminating threats and supplying resources.

Every hunt serves a purpose, whether it's securing food, protecting territories, or uncovering new discoveries about the creatures that inhabit this wild world.

Adaptability: The Key to Survival

No two hunts are the same in *Monster Hunter Wilds*. Each monster has unique behaviors, attack patterns, and environmental preferences. As a hunter, your greatest strength isn't brute force it's adaptability.

You must be able to:

- **Adjust Tactics on the Fly:** A strategy that works for one monster might fail against another. Be ready to switch up your approach mid-battle.
- **Adapt to Environmental Hazards:** Weather, terrain, and even time of day can affect your hunts. Learning how to use these factors to your advantage is critical.
- **Experiment with Equipment:** There's no one "best" weapon or armor set. Success often comes from experimenting with different builds tailored to specific hunts.

Hunters who can read the battlefield, recognize patterns, and adjust accordingly are the ones who thrive.

Team Dynamics: Your Role in Multiplayer Hunts

When hunting with others, understanding your role within a team becomes even more important. Unlike traditional RPGs with rigid class systems, *Monster Hunter Wilds* allows players to define their roles through weapon choice, gear, and playstyle. Common roles include:

- **Damage Dealers (DPS):** Focus on maximizing damage output using weapons like Great Swords, Dual Blades, or Long Swords.
- **Support Hunters:** Use hunting horns, ranged weapons, or status-inflicting gear to buff allies, heal, or control the battlefield.
- **Tanks/Disruptors:** While there's no traditional "tank" role, players with heavy armor and weapons like Lances or Hammers can control monster aggression and create openings for their team.

Good communication and synergy can turn even the toughest hunts into coordinated victories. Knowing when to lead, when to support, and when to fall back is part of mastering the hunter's role in a team setting.

The Hunter's Code: Patience, Precision, and Perseverance

At the heart of every great hunter lies a mindset shaped by three key principles:

- **Patience:** Rushing into battle recklessly leads to failure. Successful hunters observe, wait for the perfect moment, and strike with precision.
- **Precision:** Whether it's landing a critical hit on a monster's weak spot or dodging an incoming attack by a hair's breadth, precision separates skilled hunters from amateurs.
- **Perseverance:** Hunts can be long and grueling. Some monsters won't go down easily. But every defeat is a lesson, and every setback is an opportunity to grow stronger.

Mastering the hunter's role isn't about becoming invincible it's about embracing the journey, learning from your experiences, and constantly striving to improve.

CHAPTER 2: HUNTER'S ARSENAL : WEAPONS AND ARMOR

2.1 OVERVIEW OF ALL WEAPON TYPES

In *Monster Hunter Wilds*, your weapon defines not just how you fight but also how you experience the game. Each weapon type offers unique mechanics, playstyles, and strategies, catering to a wide range of players from aggressive damage dealers to tactical support hunters. Mastering your weapon is essential, as understanding its strengths, weaknesses, and optimal usage can be the difference between victory and defeat.

Great Sword: The Titan of Raw Power

The **Great Sword** is all about overwhelming force. It's a massive, heavy blade capable of dealing devastating damage with each swing. While its attacks are slow and require precise timing, a well-placed charged strike can shatter monster parts and stagger even the toughest foes.

- **Strengths:** High raw damage, excellent for breaking monster parts, powerful charged attacks.
- **Weaknesses:** Slow mobility, requires patience and precise timing, vulnerable during attack animations.
- **Ideal For:** Players who enjoy high-risk, high-reward gameplay and don't mind slower pacing.

Long Sword: Graceful Precision and Counterattacks

The **Long Sword** offers fluid, elegant combos with excellent reach. Its defining feature is the **Spirit Gauge**, which fills as you land hits, unlocking more powerful attacks. The Long Sword also has counter techniques that allow skilled players to deflect attacks and respond with devastating strikes.

- **Strengths:** High mobility, strong counterattacks, smooth combo flow.
- **Weaknesses:** Requires precise positioning, can disrupt teammates in multiplayer due to wide swings.

- **Ideal For:** Players who like fast-paced, combo-heavy combat with a stylish flair.

Sword & Shield : Versatile and Reliable

The **Sword & Shield** is a balanced weapon offering a mix of offense, defense, and item utility. It allows you to guard against attacks while maintaining high mobility. What sets it apart is the ability to use items (like potions) without sheathing your weapon, making it perfect for on-the-fly healing during intense fights.

- **Strengths:** Quick attacks, defensive capabilities, seamless item usage.
- **Weaknesses:** Lower damage compared to heavier weapons, shorter reach.
- **Ideal For:** Beginners or players who want versatility and adaptability in any situation.

Dual Blades: Blinding Speed and Elemental Fury

The **Dual Blades** are the fastest weapons in the game, specializing in rapid combos and elemental/status damage. Activating **Demon Mode** enhances attack speed and unlocks powerful combo chains, though it drains stamina quickly.

- **Strengths:** High attack speed, excellent for applying elemental/status effects, relentless combo potential.
- **Weaknesses:** Limited range, low defense, stamina-dependent.
- **Ideal For:** Players who prefer aggressive, fast-paced combat and non-stop action.

Hammer: The King of Knockouts

The **Hammer** is designed to deliver blunt force trauma. Its primary role is to deal concussive damage, making it ideal for stunning monsters by targeting their heads. Despite its size, the Hammer offers surprising mobility while charging attacks.

- **Strengths:** High stun potential, great for breaking tough parts, mobile while charging.

- **Weaknesses:** Limited range, ineffective against armored monster parts.
- **Ideal For:** Players who enjoy a straightforward, aggressive playstyle focused on staggering foes.

Hunting Horn: Supportive Yet Deadly

The **Hunting Horn** is more than just a support weapon. While it can buff teammates with songs that enhance attack power, defense, or speed, it's also capable of delivering crushing blows. Skilled Hunting Horn users can seamlessly blend offensive combos with support abilities.

- **Strengths:** Team buffs, strong blunt damage, excellent crowd control.
- **Weaknesses:** Complex mechanics, less effective when solo compared to other weapons.
- **Ideal For:** Players who enjoy a hybrid role supporting teammates while still dealing significant damage.

Lance: Unyielding Defense and Precision Strikes

The **Lance** is the ultimate defensive weapon, allowing hunters to guard against even the most powerful attacks without flinching. Its long reach and precise thrusts make it effective for targeting specific monster parts while maintaining a solid defense.

- **Strengths:** Strongest guard capabilities, great reach, precise attacks.
- **Weaknesses:** Slow movement, requires careful positioning, less flashy than other weapons.
- **Ideal For:** Players who value defense and methodical combat over flashy combos.

Gunlance: Explosive Power with a Defensive Edge

The **Gunlance** combines the defensive prowess of the Lance with explosive artillery capabilities. It features shelling attacks, charged blasts, and even a powerful **Wyvern's Fire** shot. While it shares the Lance's defensive nature, the Gunlance adds an aggressive, explosive twist to combat.

- **Strengths:** High burst damage, strong defense, explosive attacks.

- **Weaknesses:** Limited mobility, shelling reduces sharpness quickly, complex mechanics.
- **Ideal For:** Players who enjoy a defensive role but crave explosive offensive options.

Switch Axe: The Transforming Hybrid

The **Switch Axe** is a versatile weapon that switches between two forms: a long-reaching axe and a powerful sword mode. The axe form offers wide, sweeping attacks, while the sword mode deals rapid, high-damage strikes with elemental discharges.

- **Strengths:** Versatility in playstyle, strong elemental burst attacks, good range.
- **Weaknesses:** Complex to master, managing gauge levels can be challenging.
- **Ideal For:** Players who enjoy dynamic, flexible combat styles with transforming mechanics.

Charge Blade: Technical Mastery and Devastating Damage

The **Charge Blade** is a complex weapon that alternates between a sword & shield mode for defense and a massive axe mode for powerful attacks. It requires precise timing to build energy and unleash devastating **Elemental Discharge** attacks.

- **Strengths:** High burst damage potential, strong defense, versatile playstyle.
- **Weaknesses:** Steep learning curve, requires constant gauge management.
- **Ideal For:** Players who enjoy mastering technical mechanics and rewarding combos.

Insect Glaive: Aerial Acrobatics and Kinsect Synergy

The **Insect Glaive** excels in mobility, allowing hunters to vault into the air for dynamic aerial attacks. It also features a **Kinsect**, which can be sent out to extract buffs from monsters, enhancing your abilities mid-fight.

- **Strengths:** High aerial mobility, self-buffing through Kinsect extracts, fast-paced combat.

- **Weaknesses:** Lower raw damage output, requires multitasking between weapon and Kinsect management.
- **Ideal For:** Players who enjoy agile, acrobatic combat and strategic buffs.

Bow: Precision Ranged Attacks

The **Bow** offers fast, precise ranged attacks with the ability to charge shots for increased damage. It allows hunters to maintain distance while applying elemental or status effects effectively.

- **Strengths:** High mobility, strong elemental damage, versatile shot types.
- **Weaknesses:** Stamina management is crucial, less effective in close combat.
- **Ideal For:** Players who prefer ranged combat with fast, fluid movement.

Light Bowgun: Agile Firepower

The **Light Bowgun (LBG)** provides quick, agile ranged attacks with rapid-fire capabilities. It's highly versatile, supporting various ammo types for different effects, including status ailments and elemental damage.

- **Strengths:** High mobility, fast firing rate, versatile ammo selection.
- **Weaknesses:** Lower raw damage compared to heavy weapons, relies heavily on ammo management.
- **Ideal For:** Players who enjoy fast-paced, ranged combat with tactical versatility.

Heavy Bowgun : Devastating Long-Range Artillery

The **Heavy Bowgun (HBG)** is a powerhouse of ranged destruction. It deals massive damage with powerful ammo types like **Wyvernheart** and **Wyvernsnipe**. While it sacrifices mobility for firepower, its sheer destructive capability makes it a force to be reckoned with.

- **Strengths:** Unmatched ranged damage, access to powerful ammo types, long-range dominance.

- **Weaknesses:** Slow movement, vulnerable while reloading, limited in close quarters.
- **Ideal For:** Players who prefer heavy artillery and long-range sniping with devastating results.

2.2 BEST WEAPON CHOICES FOR DIFFERENT PLAYSTYLES

In *Monster Hunter Wilds*, the beauty of the hunt lies in its diversity not just in the monsters you face but in how you choose to fight them. Each hunter brings a unique approach to the battlefield, influenced by personal preferences, strategic mindsets, and combat goals. Whether you prefer relentless offense, tactical defense, supportive roles, or agile maneuvers, there's a weapon that perfectly complements your playstyle.

This section breaks down the best weapon choices based on common playstyles, helping you identify which arsenal fits your strengths and enhances your hunting experience.

OFFENSIVE PLAYSTYLE: FOR THE AGGRESSIVE DAMAGE DEALERS

If you thrive on overwhelming your enemies with raw power, rapid strikes, and relentless pressure, an offensive playstyle is your calling. The key here is maximizing damage output while maintaining control over the fight's tempo.

Best Weapon Choices:

- **Great Sword:**
  - **Why It's Great:** Massive damage potential with charged attacks that can decimate monster parts. Ideal for hunters who prefer precision over speed.
  - **Playstyle Tip:** Focus on landing fully charged slashes when monsters are downed or distracted.
- **Dual Blades:**

- **Why It's Great:** Blazing-fast attack speed with Demon Mode, perfect for stacking elemental damage and status effects.
- **Playstyle Tip:** Keep an eye on your stamina while in Demon Mode to avoid vulnerability during long combos.

- **Charge Blade:**

  - **Why It's Great:** High burst damage through Elemental Discharges after building up energy. It's versatile, allowing both defensive and aggressive stances.
  - **Playstyle Tip:** Learn to manage phials efficiently to unleash devastating Super Amped Elemental Discharge attacks.

DEFENSIVE PLAYSTYLE: FOR THE TACTICAL GUARDIANS

Hunters who prefer a calculated, methodical approach often lean toward defensive playstyles. This involves managing monster aggression, absorbing damage, and creating safe openings for counterattacks.

Best Weapon Choices:

- **Lance:**

  - **Why It's Great:** Unparalleled defensive capabilities with strong guard mechanics and precise thrust attacks.
  - **Playstyle Tip:** Master perfect guarding to conserve stamina and create opportunities for counter thrusts.

- **Gunlance:**

  - **Why It's Great:** Combines solid defense with explosive offense through shelling and Wyvern's Fire attacks.
  - **Playstyle Tip:** Use shelling strategically to deal consistent damage even when you're forced to stay defensive.

- **Sword & Shield:**

  - **Why It's Great:** Balanced offense and defense with the ability to guard while remaining mobile. Plus, you can use items without sheathing your weapon.

o **Playstyle Tip:** Utilize the shield bash for quick stuns while maintaining a solid defensive stance.

SUPPORTIVE PLAYSTYLE: FOR THE TEAM-ORIENTED HUNTERS

If your joy comes from uplifting your team, controlling the battlefield, and providing buffs, a supportive playstyle is perfect. Support hunters play a critical role, especially in multiplayer hunts, ensuring the team's survival and efficiency.

Best Weapon Choices:

- **Hunting Horn:**

  o **Why It's Great:** Provides powerful team buffs while dealing substantial blunt damage, capable of stunning monsters.
  o **Playstyle Tip:** Learn song rotations to keep buffs active, and don't underestimate your KO potential in combat.

- **Light Bowgun:**

  o **Why It's Great:** Offers versatility with status-inflicting ammo (sleep, paralysis, poison) and quick mobility to provide cover fire.
  o **Playstyle Tip:** Focus on status support, disabling monsters to create safe windows for your team's attacks.

- **Insect Glaive:**

  o **Why It's Great:** Offers aerial mobility and buffs through Kinsect extracts, making it great for controlling space and supporting ground-based teammates.
  o **Playstyle Tip:** Use your aerial agility to distract monsters, drawing attention away from vulnerable allies.

AGILE PLAYSTYLE: FOR THE SPEED ENTHUSIASTS

For hunters who live for speed, fluid movement, and quick reflexes, an agile playstyle emphasizes dodging over blocking, hit-and-run tactics, and exploiting monster weaknesses with precision strikes.

Best Weapon Choices:

- **Insect Glaive:**

    o **Why It's Great:** Unmatched aerial mobility, allowing you to vault into the air and attack from above, avoiding ground-based hazards.
    o **Playstyle Tip:** Chain aerial combos for sustained attacks while staying out of reach from dangerous ground strikes.

- **Dual Blades:**

    o **Why It's Great:** The fastest melee weapon, perfect for dashing around monsters and executing rapid combos from multiple angles.
    o **Playstyle Tip:** Use Demon Mode to stay aggressive, but manage stamina carefully to maintain mobility.
- **Bow:**

    o **Why It's Great:** High mobility with charged shots and quick dodges, allowing for sustained damage while staying out of harm's way.
    o **Playstyle Tip:** Maintain distance, exploit elemental weaknesses, and keep moving to avoid getting cornered.

RANGED PLAYSTYLE: FOR THE SNIPERS AND GUNNERS

For hunters who prefer dealing damage from a distance, controlling fights with precise shots, and avoiding close-quarters combat, the ranged playstyle offers powerful tools to dominate from afar.

Best Weapon Choices:

- **Heavy Bowgun:**

- **Why It's Great:** Delivers massive firepower with specialized ammo types, capable of decimating monsters from a distance.
- **Playstyle Tip:** Positioning is key find safe vantage points and make use of Wyvernsnipe or Wyvernheart for maximum damage.

- **Light Bowgun:**

  - **Why It's Great:** Offers quick firing rates, high mobility, and a variety of ammo for status effects and elemental damage.
  - **Playstyle Tip:** Use rapid-fire ammo to maintain pressure while dodging frequently to stay safe.
- **Bow:**

  - **Why It's Great:** A perfect blend of mobility and precision, with the ability to charge shots and apply coatings for added effects.
  - **Playstyle Tip:** Learn to charge shots efficiently and manage stamina to maintain both offensive pressure and evasive maneuvers.

BALANCED PLAYSTYLE: FOR THE JACK-OF-ALL-TRADES

Some hunters prefer flexibility able to adapt to any situation, balancing offense, defense, and support seamlessly. A balanced playstyle ensures you're never out of your element, no matter the hunt.

Best Weapon Choices:

- **Switch Axe:**

  - **Why It's Great:** Offers versatility with both wide-reaching axe attacks and high-damage sword mode.
  - **Playstyle Tip:** Learn when to switch forms for maximum efficiency axe mode for reach, sword mode for burst damage.
- **Sword & Shield:**

- **Why It's Great:** Combines quick attacks, solid defense, and item usage, making it adaptable to almost any situation.
- **Playstyle Tip:** Utilize its mobility to weave in and out of combat, applying pressure while staying safe.

- **Charge Blade:**

  - **Why It's Great:** A technical weapon that offers both strong defense and explosive offense, fitting various combat scenarios.
  - **Playstyle Tip:** Balance your time between building up energy and releasing powerful phial discharges.

2.3 CRAFTING AND UPGRADING ARMOR SETS

In *Monster Hunter Wilds*, your armor isn't just a cosmetic choice it's a critical component of your survival. The right set can bolster your defenses, enhance your strengths, and even provide you with vital resistances against the various monsters you'll face. Crafting and upgrading armor is a nuanced process, combining materials from both the environment and your fallen prey. This chapter will guide you through the essential aspects of armor crafting and upgrading, ensuring you're always ready for the challenges ahead.

CRAFTING YOUR FIRST ARMOR SET

When you first start your journey in *Monster Hunter Wilds*, crafting armor may seem like an overwhelming task. However, it's an integral part of progressing through the game, and understanding the basics will help you make informed decisions from the get-go.

Step-by-Step Crafting Process:

1. **Gathering Materials:**
   Armor sets require specific materials that are often dropped by monsters or found in various resource nodes. Each monster's parts such as scales, fangs, claws, and hides are used for different types of armor. Some materials can also be gathered from the environment, like ores and herbs.

2. **Choosing the Right Armor Set:**
   At the beginning of the game, your choices may be limited, but you can craft sets that provide a good balance of defense and elemental resistance. Later on, as you progress, you'll unlock access to more specialized sets tailored for different combat strategies.

3. **Crafting the Armor:**
   Once you have all the required materials, head to the blacksmith or crafting station in your base. Here, you can combine your collected materials to forge your first set of armor. This process may involve combining parts of the same monster or a mix of different creatures, depending on your needs.

4. **Understanding Armor Stats:**
   Armor sets have various stats, including Defense, Elemental Resistances, and Set Bonuses. Make sure to pay attention to these, as they will help you survive tougher hunts. Look for sets that provide bonuses to specific attributes that match your playstyle, such as Fire Resistance for combating fiery monsters or Affinity boosts for increased critical hit chances.

UPGRADING ARMOR FOR INCREASED STRENGTH

As you progress in *Monster Hunter Wilds*, your initial armor sets will become less effective against stronger and more dangerous monsters. Upgrading your armor is an essential part of keeping pace with the increasing difficulty of the hunts.

Upgrade Process:

1. **Using Upgrade Materials:**
   To upgrade your armor, you'll need to gather special upgrade materials. These materials are often gained by hunting stronger monsters or completing high-level quests. Some upgrades require materials from rarer monsters, so be prepared to face tougher challenges.

2. **Improving Defense and Elemental Resistances:**
   Armor upgrades generally improve the base defense value of your set, making you more resilient in combat. In addition, you can

enhance elemental resistances (e.g., fire, ice, thunder) to help mitigate the damage from certain monsters that deal elemental damage.

3. **Enhancing Set Bonuses:**
   Many armor sets come with a set bonus, granting you unique abilities or buffs when you wear the full set. Upgrading these sets can enhance these bonuses, providing significant benefits such as increased stamina regeneration, better health recovery, or boosted damage output.

4. **Maxing Out Your Armor:**
   While upgrading, you'll reach certain milestones where your armor can be maxed out, making it truly formidable. At this point, you'll have access to its best defense values and most powerful resistances. Maxing out an armor set often requires dedicated effort and materials from late-game monsters, so plan your hunts carefully

CHOOSING THE RIGHT ARMOR FOR SPECIFIC MONSTERS

Each monster in *Monster Hunter Wilds* has its own elemental and physical attacks, meaning that certain armor sets are better suited for specific encounters. Understanding these nuances will give you an edge in battle and ensure you're not caught off-guard.

Key Considerations for Armor Selection:

1. **Elemental Resistances:**
   Monsters often have elemental traits that can deal significant damage. For example, fighting a fire-breathing dragon requires armor that offers high Fire Resistance. Pay attention to the elemental attacks of the monsters you're targeting and equip armor that offers the best protection.

2. **Monster-Specific Armor Sets:**
   Some armor sets are designed specifically to counter certain monsters. For instance, an armor set crafted from materials dropped by a water-based monster might offer high Water

Resistance, making it ideal for fighting other aquatic creatures.

3. **Physical Defense vs. Elemental Resistance:**
   While physical defense is essential for general survival, some encounters require a specific focus on elemental resistances. If you're up against a monster known for its devastating elemental attacks, prioritize armor that can reduce the damage from that element, even if it means sacrificing a bit of physical defense.

4. **Upgrading for Monster Weaknesses:**
   Upgrading your armor for specific monster encounters can make a big difference. Look for armor that complements the monster's weaknesses, whether it's elemental resistance or reducing the damage from particular attacks.

SPECIAL ARMOR SETS AND ENDGAME GEAR

As you progress to the endgame, the crafting and upgrading system becomes more complex, offering armor sets that are specifically designed for high-level hunts and extreme challenges. These sets come with powerful attributes and resistances that can turn the tide of battle in your favor.

Notable Endgame Armor Sets:

1. **Legendary Sets:**
   These sets are often tied to the hardest monsters in the game. They provide high defense, powerful set bonuses, and enhanced resistances. Legendary armor can give you the edge you need in the toughest endgame hunts.

2. **Monster-Specific Armor Bonuses:**
   Some armor sets offer bonuses that help you counter specific boss fights or high-level monster traits. For example, armor with a bonus to stun resistance can be invaluable when facing monsters that frequently use stunning moves.

3. **Customizing Armor for Max Efficiency:**
   As you reach the highest levels of the game, you'll be able to further refine your armor's attributes using unique upgrade materials. These enhancements allow for increased survivability

and additional stat boosts, making your hunter an unstoppable force.

4. **Endgame Crafting Materials:**
   To craft or upgrade the best armor, you'll need rare and powerful materials dropped from the hardest monsters. These materials are often hard to come by, requiring multiple successful hunts or participation in multiplayer sessions to gather enough resources for your final set.

2.4 HIDDEN WEAPON SKILLS AND HOW TO UNLOCK THEM

In *Monster Hunter Wilds*, the weapons at your disposal are far more than just tools for combat; they are your key to mastering the game's intricate battle system. While the base abilities and combos of each weapon are widely known, hidden weapon skills can take your fighting techniques to the next level. These skills often unlock through specific conditions, such as defeating certain monsters, reaching specific milestones, or mastering particular playstyles.

This chapter will guide you through the process of unlocking hidden weapon skills and provide you with the knowledge to fully harness the power of your weapon choices. Whether you're using a greatsword, bow, or dual blades, these hidden abilities can give you a distinct advantage in the heat of battle.

UNLOCKING HIDDEN SKILLS THROUGH WEAPON MASTERY

One of the most common ways to unlock hidden weapon skills is through the progression and mastery of specific weapons. As you use a particular weapon in hunts, your proficiency with it improves, and hidden skills become available.

Mastery Progression:

1. **Weapon Use and Proficiency:**
   Each time you wield a weapon in combat, you increase your

proficiency with that weapon. The more you use a weapon, the more you unlock its potential. As you achieve higher levels of weapon proficiency, new skills or enhancements become available, often requiring a specific number of attacks or combos executed during hunts.

2. **Weapon Rank and Skill Tiers:**
   Weapons in *Monster Hunter Wilds* come with different rank tiers, each offering the possibility to unlock hidden skills. These skills are often more powerful versions of the weapon's base abilities or unique moves that give you more tactical advantages. Reaching higher ranks often unlocks additional slots for skill customization.

3. **Focus on Specific Combos:**
   Many hidden skills are tied to executing certain combos or actions during hunts. For instance, certain skills may be unlocked after performing a series of attacks within a time limit or activating special moves at critical moments. Paying attention to these combos and practicing them during combat will gradually unlock new abilities.

4. **Weapon-Specific Achievements:**
   In some cases, hidden skills are tied to completing specific achievements related to your weapon, such as breaking parts of monsters in a particular way or executing perfect dodges after certain attacks. These milestones can be tracked in your achievement log, giving you a clear path to follow for unlocking these advanced skills.

UNLOCKING HIDDEN SKILLS BY DEFEATING MONSTERS

In *Monster Hunter Wilds*, many hidden weapon skills are tied to the monsters you hunt. Defeating particular creatures will unlock specific abilities that complement your weapon's strengths and help you tailor your playstyle to counter various enemies.

How Monster Hunts Unlock Skills:

1. **Monster-Specific Skills:**
   Certain monsters drop unique materials that are tied to special

weapon abilities. For example, defeating a tough fire-breathing monster might unlock fire-infused attacks for your weapons, allowing you to deal elemental damage with your strikes. Other monsters might grant new moves, such as charged attacks or more powerful combos, as part of their reward.

2. **Targeting Weaknesses for Hidden Skills:**
   Some hidden skills are unlocked by exploiting a monster's particular weakness. For example, monsters with strong elemental defenses might require you to use specific elemental weapons or attacks in precise ways. Mastering these techniques and successfully defeating these creatures will unlock hidden skills that give you an edge in future hunts.

3. **High-Level Hunts and Rare Monsters:**
   The most potent hidden skills are often unlocked after you defeat rare, high-level, or endgame monsters. These hunts are challenging but offer great rewards in the form of advanced weapon skills. These skills can drastically change how you approach combat and allow you to become more versatile in the field.

4. **Material Unlocks:**
   Upon defeating a monster, you can collect rare parts that are used not only for crafting and upgrading your gear but also for unlocking specific weapon skills. The more difficult the monster, the rarer the materials, and the more powerful the hidden weapon skill that can be unlocked.

CUSTOMIZATION AND WEAPON SKILL TREE

As you progress through the game, you'll unlock the ability to further customize your weapons and their abilities through the weapon skill tree. This system allows you to specialize your weapon in a way that complements your combat style, adding an extra layer of depth to your gameplay.

Weapon Skill Tree Overview:

1. **Unlocking Branches and Nodes:**
   Every weapon has its own skill tree, with various nodes

representing different abilities. As you unlock these nodes, you'll gain access to new skills, such as faster attack speeds, enhanced elemental damage, or even entirely new moves that change the flow of combat. The skill tree is also where you can unlock the hidden skills tied to particular weapons or monsters.

2. **Resource Allocation:**
   To unlock these skills, you need to invest specific resources, such as monster materials or in-game currency. This means that unlocking hidden skills requires a balance of time spent hunting and resource management. Focus on gathering the necessary materials to unlock the specific skills that best suit your playstyle.

3. **Skill Synergies:**
   Many hidden weapon skills work best when paired with certain abilities from other weapons or armor sets. Experiment with different combinations of skills to discover synergies that maximize your combat efficiency. Some skills complement elemental attacks, while others enhance critical hit chances or stamina regeneration, giving you a variety of ways to approach battle.

4. **Advanced Skill Customization:**
   At the highest levels, you'll be able to completely customize your weapon's skill set, including hidden abilities. This allows you to build a weapon that perfectly matches your preferred tactics, whether that's dealing rapid, high-damage combos or infusing your strikes with elemental power. Take the time to explore the full skill tree to unlock all the hidden potential of your weapons.

TIPS FOR UNLOCKING ALL HIDDEN WEAPON SKILLS

Unlocking hidden weapon skills takes time, dedication, and mastery over your weapon of choice. Here are some tips to ensure you unlock every possible skill available:

1. **Experiment with Weapon Types:**
   Don't focus on just one weapon type. Experimenting with different weapon classes will expose you to different hidden skills,

some of which might better complement your style of combat.

2. **Focus on Weapon Mastery:**
   Level up your weapon proficiency by using it consistently in hunts. The more you use a weapon, the closer you get to unlocking its hidden skills.

3. **Pay Attention to Achievements and Milestones:**
   Keep track of in-game achievements and milestones that are tied to specific weapon skills. Often, hidden skills are unlocked through these conditions, so keeping an eye on them will guide you toward your goal.

4. **Join Multiplayer Hunts:**
   Some of the rarest and most challenging monsters are easier to take down in multiplayer sessions. Joining groups allows you to access new monsters and unlock rare skills faster than if you were hunting alone.

CHAPTER 3: MASTERING COMBAT MECHANICS

3.1 UNDERSTANDING THE COMBAT SYSTEM AND CONTROLS

In *Monster Hunter Wilds*, the combat system is as dynamic and multifaceted as the creatures you'll be hunting. Whether you're going solo or teaming up with friends in multiplayer, mastering the combat mechanics is essential for survival. This chapter breaks down the core aspects of combat, helping you understand how to engage in smooth, fluid, and strategic battles against the most fearsome monsters.

Combat Basics: The Hunter's Playstyle

The key to success in *Monster Hunter Wilds* lies in your ability to adapt to different combat scenarios. Each weapon class offers a distinct playstyle, from fast-paced, close-quarters combat to ranged, tactical assault. Understanding these differences will allow you to make the most of your arsenal and develop a combat strategy tailored to your preferences.

Melee Combat: Up Close and Personal:

- Melee weapons are for hunters who prefer to get in the thick of the action. The Greatsword, Longsword, and Dual Blades are designed for hunters who like to close the gap and deal damage directly to the monster.
- Melee combat requires mastering timing whether it's blocking, dodging, or delivering powerful combos, every action you take must be precise.
- Focus on learning each weapon's attack combos and how to properly chain them together for maximum damage. Mastering evasion and counterattacks will also be key to surviving in tight situations.

Ranged Combat: Precision from a Distance:

- If you prefer attacking from a safe distance, ranged weapons like the Bow, Light Bowgun, and Heavy Bowgun are your go-to. These weapons require a more calculated approach to combat, where accuracy and positioning are crucial.

- The combat flow with ranged weapons demands precision in aiming, timing when to fire, and knowing when to reposition to avoid being overwhelmed by a monster's attacks.

Controls Breakdown: From Hunter to Master

The controls in *Monster Hunter Wilds* are intuitive yet deep, allowing for flexibility in how you approach combat. Whether you're using a controller or mouse and keyboard, it's important to get comfortable with the mechanics that govern every action, from attacking to dodging to using items.

Basic Controls for Combat:

1. **Movement and Stamina:**

   o   In combat, your movement is directly tied to your stamina. Every action, from dodging to sprinting, depletes stamina, so managing your energy is vital to avoid getting caught off guard. Learn to pace yourself and watch your stamina bar to know when you can go all-out and when you should back off to recharge.

2. **Attacks and Combos:**

   o   Every weapon has a basic set of attacks that can be chained into powerful combos. Mastering these attack sequences allows you to dish out high damage while maintaining control over the battlefield. Pay close attention to your weapon's move list and the timing of each attack to maximize your effectiveness.

3. **Dodge and Evasion:**

   o   Dodging is one of the most crucial mechanics in *Monster Hunter Wilds*. Understanding the direction and timing of monster attacks is key to evading damage. With a few practice sessions, you'll learn how to roll or dash out of the way at just the right moment to avoid getting hit while also positioning yourself for the next attack.

4. **Guarding and Counterattacking:**

    o Some weapons, like the Greatsword and Shield, offer excellent defensive capabilities. Learning how to guard and counterattack is critical for surviving tough monster encounters. A well-timed block or counterattack can open up the enemy for devastating follow-up hits.

Advanced Combat Actions:

1. **Special Moves and Abilities:**

    o Every weapon type has unique special moves or abilities that can turn the tide of battle. Whether it's the Longsword's Spirit Slash or the Bow's Charge Shots, understanding when and how to use these skills can make a huge difference. These abilities often have a cooldown, so using them strategically is key to winning battles efficiently.

2. **Aiming and Precision:**

    o For ranged weapons, controlling your aim is essential. The aiming reticle helps you lock on to your target, but advanced players learn how to adjust their shots mid-flight for greater accuracy, especially when dealing with moving monsters or attacking weak points.

3. **Weapon Sheathing and Switching:**

    o Quickly sheathing and unsheathing your weapon can often mean the difference between life and death in the heat of battle. Mastering the timing for switching between weapons, or using items while keeping an eye on your surroundings, adds versatility to your combat style.

4. **Environmental Interactions:**

    o The terrain in *Monster Hunter Wilds* is more than just background scenery it's an integral part of combat. Learn to use the environment to your advantage, whether it's hiding behind a rock to recover health, using trees as cover from ranged attacks, or triggering environmental hazards to deal damage to your foes.

Combat Strategy and Preparation:

Before you even engage in a fight, you need to prepare yourself. Gathering the right gear, selecting the best weapon, and considering your monster's behavior all play a role in your success.

Pre-Hunt Preparations:

1. **Selecting the Right Weapon:**

    o Think about your combat style and the type of monster you'll be hunting. If you're facing a large, slow-moving beast, a heavy weapon like the Greatsword might be more beneficial. If you're going after a smaller, more agile monster, a faster weapon like the Dual Blades could give you the upper hand.

2. **Picking the Right Armor and Items:**

    o Equip yourself with armor that enhances your combat abilities. Consider which stats (defense, elemental resistance, etc.) will be most helpful for the battle ahead. Don't forget to bring along useful items like traps, bombs, or healing potions to aid you during the hunt.

In-Combat Strategy:

1. **Monster Behavior and Patterns:**

    o Each monster has its own attack patterns. Observing their movements and recognizing when they're about to strike allows you to avoid damage and counterattack effectively. Taking the time to learn how each monster moves and reacts to your attacks will allow you to plan your strategy.

2. **Managing Aggression:**

    o In some fights, it's better to play the waiting game. Don't rush in; instead, wait for the monster to make a move before countering. Timing your attacks and not getting too greedy can save you from leaving yourself open to deadly strikes.

3.2 BEST STRATEGIES FOR SOLO AND CO-OP HUNTS

Whether you're setting out on your own in *Monster Hunter Wilds* or teaming up with friends in a co-op hunt, success depends on how well you adapt to each situation. Solo hunts demand different tactics than multiplayer hunts, as the challenges and available resources vary significantly. This section explores the best strategies for both solo and co-op hunts, ensuring you're equipped to take down any monster that stands in your way.

Solo Hunts: Strategies for the Lone Hunter

Solo hunts offer a more intimate experience, allowing you to focus on your combat abilities and tactics without relying on teammates. However, this comes with its own set of challenges, especially when facing larger and more aggressive monsters. Here are some essential strategies to help you thrive in solo hunts:

1. Prepare for Longevity:

In solo hunts, it's crucial to be prepared for longer battles, as you won't have anyone to rely on for healing or support. Stock up on healing items, buffs, and traps before heading out. Make sure to bring the right armor that balances defense and mobility. You'll also want to bring tools like Flash Pods or Trap Tools to incapacitate monsters for easy damage dealing.

2. Master Monster Behavior and Weaknesses:

Solo hunting is all about patience and observation. Before engaging, take time to study the monster's attack patterns and weaknesses. Knowing when to strike and when to dodge is vital. Use your first few moments in the fight to gauge the monster's behavior learn its movements, timing, and the signs that indicate a heavy attack is incoming.

3. Manage Your Stamina and Positioning:

Since you'll be the only one dealing damage, keeping track of your stamina is critical. If you're using a melee weapon, like the Greatsword or Hammer, learn how to manage your stamina so you can avoid exhaustion during a fight. Keep your distance when your stamina is low, or switch to ranged attacks if you need to regain some energy. Additionally, positioning yourself behind the monster can help you land hits without exposing yourself to dangerous attacks.

4. Use Hit-and-Run Tactics:

Solo hunters often have to rely on hit-and-run tactics, especially when facing faster monsters. Avoid trying to tank all the damage and instead focus on attacking when the monster's defenses are down. Wait for an opening, strike quickly, and retreat before the monster can retaliate. This will help you whittle down its health without risking an unnecessary hit.

Co-op Hunts: Strategies for Group Success

Co-op hunts are an entirely different beast. With multiple hunters, you have the opportunity to coordinate, strategize, and maximize damage output. However, this requires effective teamwork to ensure everyone plays their part. Here's how to succeed in a co-op hunt:

1. Coordinate Weapon Choices:

In a co-op hunt, having a balanced team is key to success. Ideally, each player should choose a weapon that complements others' playstyles. For example, if one player uses a ranged weapon like the Light Bowgun, another player could opt for a melee weapon like the Sword and Shield for close-quarters combat. Having a mix of damage types (physical, elemental, etc.) allows the team to exploit the monster's weaknesses more effectively.

2. Focus on Roles and Support:

Each member of your team should have a clear role. Some players will deal the majority of the damage, while others may focus on healing, buffing, or controlling the monster. It's vital that all players understand their roles before the hunt begins. If you're the support player, make sure you carry potions, traps, and healing items to assist your teammates. If you're the damage dealer, focus on positioning and keeping pressure on the monster at all times.

3. Communication and Timing:

In co-op hunts, communication is crucial. Whether you're using voice chat or a ping system, staying in sync with your team can mean the difference between victory and defeat. Let your team know when you're about to use your special abilities, when you need healing, or when the monster is about to launch an attack. Coordinating actions like using traps or placing status ailments can set up devastating attacks that are harder to pull off on your own.

4. Take Advantage of the Monster's Weaknesses:

When hunting as a group, you'll have more opportunities to exploit the monster's weaknesses. With multiple players attacking from different angles, monsters can be staggered more easily, leaving them open to critical hits. Try to break the monster's parts (such as its tail or wings) during the hunt, as this not only weakens it but also provides valuable materials for crafting better gear. A good strategy is to have one player focus on breaking parts while others deal consistent damage to the monster.

Mixed Strategies: Transitioning Between Solo and Co-op Hunts

Some situations in *Monster Hunter Wilds* may require you to switch between solo and co-op hunts. For example, you might start a hunt alone, but halfway through, another hunter joins in. In these cases, it's important to be flexible and adapt your tactics.

1. Don't Overextend:

Whether you're playing solo or with a team, one rule remains the same: don't overextend yourself. If you're alone, don't try to take on a monster that's too strong without preparation. Similarly, in co-op, ensure everyone is on the same page before rushing into a fight. Overcommitting can lead to mistakes and leave you exposed to unnecessary damage.

2. Stay Mobile and Adaptable:

In both solo and co-op hunts, mobility is crucial. When you're hunting alone, you need to be nimble, using your surroundings to your advantage. When hunting in a group, the dynamics can change quickly. Monsters may shift their focus from one player to another, or the group's positioning may change over time. Stay adaptable and be ready to adjust your strategy as needed.

3.3 ADVANCED DODGING, PARRYING, AND COUNTER TECHNIQUES

In *Monster Hunter Wilds*, mastering advanced dodging, parrying, and counter techniques is crucial to elevating your combat skills. These defensive maneuvers allow you to avoid taking damage, create openings for powerful attacks, and gain an upper hand against the most challenging monsters. This section dives deep into these techniques, explaining how to execute them effectively and how to incorporate them into your strategy.

Dodging: Mastering Evasion and Timing

Dodging is one of the fundamental defensive techniques in *Monster Hunter Wilds*. A well-timed dodge can save you from devastating attacks, and with the right timing, it can even open up opportunities for counterattacks.

1. **Perfect Dodge Timing:** The key to perfect dodging is learning the attack patterns of monsters. The best time to dodge is right before the attack lands, allowing you to avoid the damage and simultaneously create a window to retaliate. Practice your timing by observing the monster's movements when you see an attack about to land, perform a quick dodge to the side or backwards. Timing is critical; dodging too early or too late can leave you vulnerable.

2. **Dodging Through Attacks:** Some weapons, such as the Sword and Shield or the Insect Glaive, allow you to dodge through an attack. This means you'll evade the impact by dodging directly into the attack's path. This technique requires precision and confidence, as it lets you stay close to the monster, ensuring you can immediately follow up with your own attack once the dodge is completed.

3. **Dodge and Sprint Combo:** Dodging into a sprint allows you to immediately reposition yourself after evading an attack. This is particularly useful when dealing with fast-moving monsters or when you need to quickly create space between yourself and the target. The sprint is especially effective in solo hunts where you

might need to create distance before healing or regrouping with your teammates.

4. **Dodge Roll vs. Quickstep:** Depending on your weapon and playstyle, you can either use the dodge roll or quickstep. The dodge roll is generally better for slower, heavier weapons, allowing you to cover more distance with less stamina consumption. The quickstep, on the other hand, is ideal for faster weapons or more mobile hunters, allowing you to slip past attacks and quickly adjust your position.

Parrying: Deflecting Attacks with Precision

Parrying is an advanced technique that allows you to block and deflect an enemy's attack while remaining in control of your position. Mastering parrying is especially valuable for weapons like the Sword and Shield, Gunlance, or Lance, which offer defensive capabilities.

1. **Timing the Parry:** To execute a successful parry, you must time it perfectly with the monster's attack. Parrying too early or too late will either result in a failed parry or worse, leave you open to the attack. Focus on reading the monster's movements and try to anticipate its strikes. When you successfully parry, the monster will be briefly staggered, leaving it open for a counterattack.

2. **Weapons with Built-in Parry Mechanics:** Certain weapons come with parrying abilities built into their movesets. For example, the Gunlance's shield can block incoming attacks, and the Lance allows for precise parrying with its long reach. Practice with these weapons to make the most out of their defensive capabilities. Keep in mind that while parrying, your stamina will be drained, so you need to gauge how many parries you can execute before needing to back off.

3. **Perfect Parry:** Some monsters have attacks that, when perfectly parried, can leave them open for devastating combos. A perfect parry not only deflects the attack but also momentarily stuns the enemy, allowing you to land powerful blows. Learn to identify these moments when a monster is about to launch its hardest strike, position yourself for the perfect parry and capitalize on the opening.

4. **Parry and Counter Combos:** After successfully parrying an attack, you're in the perfect position to launch a counterattack. This is especially important when facing large, slow-moving monsters. A quick counterattack after a parry can deal substantial damage, so practice chaining these combos for maximum impact. Parry, then immediately follow up with a charged attack or a fast combo to punish the monster for its missed strike.

Counter Techniques: Turning the Tables

Countering is the art of using your enemy's attack against them, turning their momentum into an opportunity for a devastating strike. Counter techniques are best performed with precision and mastery, requiring you to recognize when a monster's attack leaves it vulnerable.

1. **Reading Monster Attack Patterns:** To land a successful counterattack, it's essential to read the monster's movements and understand when it's about to launch a critical strike. The key to effective countering is identifying the specific moments when a monster is vulnerable usually after a heavy attack or when it's recovering from an offensive move. Once you've identified the right moment, position yourself to strike and wait for the opening.

2. **Counter Moves for Different Weapons:** Certain weapons offer unique counter abilities, such as the Greatsword's "True Charge Slash" or the Dual Blades' "Demon Mode." These moves allow you to absorb or deflect incoming attacks while dealing damage in return. For instance, the Greatsword can counter an attack by charging up a powerful blow just before the monster strikes, turning the tables and punishing the enemy with devastating power.

3. **Timing and Stamina Management for Counters:** Just like with dodging and parrying, timing is crucial for counter techniques. Counters usually require precise timing, but they also rely on stamina management. Be sure to conserve enough stamina to execute a successful counter. Overexerting yourself will leave you vulnerable to attacks, and you may miss the opportunity for a counter. Mastering your stamina usage will help you maintain your readiness to perform counters at critical moments.

4. **Countering with Traps and Status Effects:** Some monsters are more susceptible to traps and status effects, which can make your counters even more effective. For example, if a monster is stunned or trapped, it's a perfect time to launch a counterattack. Similarly, if you've applied poison or paralysis to a monster, its movements may become sluggish, giving you a better chance to land critical hits during your counterattack.

3.4 HOW TO HANDLE LARGE AND AGGRESSIVE MONSTERS

When hunting in *Monster Hunter Wilds*, one of the most exhilarating yet challenging aspects of the game is facing off against large and aggressive monsters. These behemoths often possess overwhelming strength, fast attack patterns, and devastating special moves that can easily overwhelm an unprepared hunter. Knowing how to handle them effectively is crucial to your success. This section will explore strategies for surviving and thriving when taking on these powerful foes.

1. Recognizing Attack Patterns and Weaknesses

Before diving into combat with a large monster, it's essential to understand its attack patterns and weaknesses. Most large monsters have several key moves that can be predicted, giving you the opportunity to evade or counterattack effectively.

1. **Study the Monster's Behavior:** Each large monster has a set of telltale signs that precede its most dangerous attacks. Learn to recognize these visual and audio cues whether it's a roar, a stance change, or a wind-up for a special move. Once you've identified these patterns, you'll be able to dodge or block at the right time, avoiding heavy damage.

2. **Target Weak Points:** All monsters have specific weak points whether it's their head, tail, wings, or limbs. For large monsters, focusing on these weak points not only helps you deal more damage but may also trigger status effects like paralysis, poison, or breaking parts of the monster. Always aim for these points, especially when a monster is staggering or otherwise vulnerable after a missed attack.

3. **Elemental and Status Weaknesses:** Many large monsters have elemental or status effect vulnerabilities. Fire, water, ice, and lightning attacks can significantly damage certain monsters, while poison, paralysis, and sleep can provide you with a brief window to attack without retaliation. Check your monster's elemental weaknesses before heading into battle and tailor your weapon and armor to exploit those weaknesses.

2. Managing Your Positioning and Mobility

Handling large monsters requires precise positioning and constant mobility to avoid getting caught in their devastating attacks. Simply charging headfirst into battle is a recipe for disaster, so understanding where to be and when to move is essential.

1. **Staying Behind the Monster:** Large monsters often rely on powerful frontal attacks, leaving their rear and sides more vulnerable. By staying behind the monster, you reduce your chances of getting hit by sweeping or cone-shaped attacks. Position yourself in a way that allows you to land attacks on the monster's weak points while avoiding its most dangerous moves.

2. **Utilizing the Terrain:** The environment can be your best friend when fighting large monsters. Use ledges, rocks, trees, or other terrain features to your advantage. For example, some monsters are susceptible to being stunned or trapped by environmental hazards like falling rocks or pits. Staying on higher ground may also provide a safer vantage point to avoid incoming attacks.

3. **Mobility is Key:** Large monsters are slow-moving but devastatingly powerful. Constant movement is crucial to staying alive. Dodge and roll to avoid monster swipes and charged-up attacks, and don't be afraid to back away when necessary. Always watch the monster's movements, and when an attack seems imminent, focus on dodging and then repositioning for your next strike.

4. **Managing Stamina:** Large monster fights are long and require a lot of stamina management. Overexerting yourself by dodging too many times or attacking recklessly can leave you vulnerable. Prioritize stamina regeneration by avoiding overuse of heavy

attacks and using items like stamina-restoring potions when necessary.

3. Teamwork and Co-op Strategy

When hunting large monsters, especially in multiplayer or co-op mode, teamwork becomes an essential component for success. Coordinating with your team can not only maximize damage output but also ensure that the group remains intact and well-prepared throughout the battle.

1. **Distribute Roles Within the Team:** Assign specific roles to each member of your team to streamline the hunt. For instance, designate one hunter to focus on weakening the monster's limbs while another focuses on dealing damage to its head. Having someone focused on healing or providing buffs with support items can make a huge difference during longer battles. Communicate effectively to avoid overlapping efforts.

2. **Aggro Control and Distraction:** Some large monsters have a tendency to target the player who deals the most damage or makes the most noise. This is where aggro control becomes important. The tankiest players (often those using heavy weapons or shields) should draw the monster's attention away from the more vulnerable hunters, allowing them to focus on damage dealing. Alternatively, use traps or environmental hazards to redirect the monster's attention temporarily.

3. **Synchronize Attacks:** Large monsters usually have attack patterns that leave them vulnerable at certain points. Synchronize your team's attacks to capitalize on these openings. For example, when a monster is about to charge or prepare for a big attack, ensure your team is in position to unleash coordinated attacks, aiming for weak points at the same time.

4. **Healing and Buffing Together:** During co-op hunts, make sure the team communicates about healing needs and buffs. Large monsters can cause heavy damage, and while your team members focus on offense, others should be ready to heal or buff using items like potions, traps, or status effect-laden tools (e.g., flash bombs). Staying on top of your team's health ensures that no one is left behind during critical moments.

4. Patience and Persistence: Endurance Against Large Monsters

Fighting large monsters in *Monster Hunter Wilds* is not a race; it's a test of endurance. These foes can take a lot of hits, and it's important to maintain your focus and stamina over the course of a prolonged battle.

1. **Don't Rush:** Large monsters can be intimidating due to their size and power, but trying to rush through the fight by spamming attacks is a sure way to fail. Instead, focus on your timing wait for the right moment to strike, and make sure each attack counts. It's about making the battle last as long as it needs to while carefully conserving your resources.

2. **Prepare for a Marathon, Not a Sprint:** Battles against large monsters often take time, requiring you to remain patient and deliberate. Make sure you're properly prepared with plenty of healing items, buffs, and traps. Keep your cool, even if the fight drags on longer than expected. If your stamina or health is running low, don't be afraid to pull back, regroup, and heal. A calm hunter is a victorious hunter.

3. **Watch for Exhaustion:** Many large monsters will enter an exhausted state after a long battle, where they become slower and less aggressive. This is the perfect time to unload your heaviest attacks. Keep track of the monster's stamina and behavior to capitalize on this opportunity.

4. **Adapt as the Battle Progresses:** As you chip away at the monster's health, it may change its attack behavior, become more aggressive, or even enter an enraged state. Be ready to adapt to these changes by adjusting your positioning, healing, and strategy. Don't be discouraged by setbacks adaptation is key to success.

CHAPTER 4: MONSTER ENCYCLOPEDIA

4.1 PROFILES OF MAJOR MONSTERS AND THEIR WEAKNESSES

Monster Hunter Wilds is home to an expansive world filled with terrifying and awe-inspiring creatures. As a hunter, your journey will bring you face-to-face with a variety of monsters, each possessing unique abilities, behaviors, and weaknesses. Understanding these creatures is essential for your survival and success in the game. In this chapter, we will break down the major monsters you will encounter, detailing their profiles and revealing their weaknesses so you can strategically prepare for every hunt.

In *Monster Hunter Wilds*, monsters come in all shapes and sizes, from massive, lumbering giants to swift, aerial predators. Each monster has a distinct set of traits, elemental affinities, and behavior patterns. Knowing how to exploit their weaknesses can make all the difference between a successful hunt and a painful defeat. Let's dive into the profiles of some of the most formidable creatures you'll encounter in your travels.

1. Rathalos : The King of the Skies

- **Overview:** Rathalos is one of the most iconic monsters in the *Monster Hunter* series, known for its fierce aerial combat and fiery attacks. As a flying wyvern, Rathalos can cover vast distances in the air, bombarding hunters from above with fire-based attacks and high-speed charges. Its large wings and sharp claws make it a fearsome opponent, both in the sky and on the ground.

- **Weaknesses:** Rathalos is particularly vulnerable to **Water** and **Dragon** attacks. Aiming for its head or tail will deal significant damage, especially when it is in a vulnerable state after a missed aerial strike or landing. Be wary of its fire-based breath, and use water-based weapons or elemental traps to neutralize its fiery prowess. Additionally, its legs can be broken to reduce its mobility.

2. Diablos: The Desert Terror

- **Overview:** Diablos is a fearsome monster known for its sheer brute strength and aggressive tendencies. Found primarily in the desert, this large, horned monster uses its massive tusks to tunnel underground and ambush its prey. When enraged, it becomes even more dangerous, charging at hunters with relentless fury. Diablos is notorious for its ability to control the battlefield with its massive horns and wide-reaching attacks.

- **Weaknesses:** Diablos is weak to **Water** and **Ice** attacks. Its head is a prime target for dealing massive damage, as well as its tail, which can be severed to prevent it from using its powerful charging attacks. While its thick body is difficult to penetrate, aiming for its weak points particularly when it's tired from charging can turn the tide of battle in your favor. Also, **Thunder** weapons are effective against it during specific parts of the fight when its guard is down.

3. Nargacuga : The Stealthy Night Stalker

- **Overview:** Nargacuga is a sleek, agile monster that relies on speed and stealth to take down its prey. With its jet-black fur and highly efficient tail, this monster is known for its quick movements and vicious tail swipes. Nargacuga often hides in the shadows, making it difficult for hunters to track. Its quick leaping attacks can disorient even the most experienced hunters, so staying on your toes is a must.

- **Weaknesses:** Nargacuga is weak to **Fire** and **Ice** attacks. Its tail, in particular, is a critical weak spot, and severing it can significantly reduce the monster's ability to deal damage. The head is also a vulnerable target, but it's best approached when the monster is distracted or stunned. Additionally, **Dragon** attacks can bypass its agility, dealing considerable damage when timed correctly.

4. Tygrix : The Roaring Beast of the Swamp

- **Overview:** Tygrix is a massive, swamp-dwelling brute that combines raw power with an overwhelming roar. Its scaly hide makes it resistant to most forms of physical damage, but its slow movements make it vulnerable to careful, calculated attacks. Tygrix relies on its massive tail to sweep hunters away, and its heavy body allows it to crush anything in its path.

- **Weaknesses:** Tygrix is vulnerable to **Thunder** and **Water** attacks. Its head is the most critical weak point, and focusing your efforts on hitting this spot can make the fight much easier. Additionally, when Tygrix rears back for a devastating charge, its legs become a secondary weak point. Breaking these legs can cause the beast to stumble, reducing its mobility and giving hunters an opportunity to attack.

5. Zinogre : The Thunder Beast

- **Overview:** Zinogre is a large, wolf-like monster that harnesses the power of electricity to enhance its attacks. Often seen charging up electrical energy in its body, it can deliver lightning-infused strikes that can paralyze hunters or deal devastating damage. Zinogre is known for its speed and agility, and its ability to leap and deliver powerful tail whips makes it a challenging foe to pin down.

- **Weaknesses:** Zinogre is highly susceptible to **Water** and **Ice** attacks. Its head is the primary target for critical damage, but you'll need to focus on weakening its charge by attacking its legs and back. Once Zinogre has fully charged up its electrical energy, it becomes more dangerous, so taking the opportunity to deal damage when it's weakened by paralysis or after a missed strike can significantly shorten the battle.

6. Lagiacrus : The Sea Serpent

- **Overview:** Lagiacrus is a massive sea serpent that terrorizes the deep oceans and is one of the most iconic aquatic monsters in the *Monster Hunter* series. Using its long, sinuous body and powerful tail, Lagiacrus can create massive waves and launch devastating water-based attacks. While it may seem slow on land, this monster is far more agile and aggressive underwater, making it a true force to be reckoned with in its natural habitat.

- **Weaknesses:** Lagiacrus is most vulnerable to **Thunder** and **Dragon** attacks. The head and tail are its weakest points, but during underwater fights, hitting these weak points can be more difficult. The Lagiacrus is highly susceptible to **Thunder** weapons, so it's important to bring along weapons that can deal high electrical damage to exploit this vulnerability.

7. Brachydios : The Explosive Brute

- **Overview:** Brachydios is a massive, slime-covered brute whose primary method of attack involves using its explosive, slime-covered fists. This monster has an explosive nature literally leaving a trail of destruction in its wake. Its unpredictable movement patterns and explosive attacks make it a formidable opponent, but its ability to be stunned and controlled with the right strategy allows skilled hunters to counter its volatility.

- **Weaknesses:** Brachydios is vulnerable to **Water** and **Ice** attacks. Its head and arms are weak points to target, with the head being the most crucial area for dealing significant damage. When the slime covering its body begins to glow, it's time to back away, as it's preparing to unleash a powerful explosion. Use **Fire** attacks to ignite the slime and deal additional damage.

8. Rathian : The Queen of the Land

- **Overview:** Rathian is the female counterpart to Rathalos and is equally as dangerous. Known as the "Queen of the Land," Rathian is heavily armored and adept at both aerial and terrestrial combat. Its poison-infused tail and fiery breath make it a deadly foe, and hunters must be prepared for both its aggressive attacks and its ability to control the battlefield with poison.

- **Weaknesses:** Rathian is weak to **Water** and **Ice** attacks. The head and tail are the most vulnerable spots, and severing its tail can greatly reduce its range of poison-infused attacks. When Rathian is airborne, it's a prime opportunity to deal damage to its head, but timing your attacks carefully is key to avoiding its poison and fiery breath.

4.2 HOW TO TRACK AND HUNT RARE MONSTERS

In *Monster Hunter Wilds*, rare monsters are among the most challenging and rewarding creatures to hunt. These elusive beasts are often hidden in specific locations, require special strategies to locate, and boast unique abilities and behavior that set them apart from the regular monsters. Tracking and hunting them down requires a keen eye, patience, and preparation. This section will guide you through the process of finding rare monsters, what to expect when you encounter them, and how to effectively take them down.

1. Understanding the Criteria for Rare Monsters

Before setting out to hunt a rare monster, it's important to know how to identify one and what makes them stand out. Rare monsters often have different characteristics compared to the common creatures in the game:

- **Special Behavior Patterns:** Rare monsters may have different attack patterns, more aggressive tendencies, or unique movement abilities that make them harder to track and defeat. Some may also be more sensitive to environmental factors like weather or time of day.

- **Unique Markings and Features:** Look for visual clues like glowing body parts, different-colored scales, or distinctive environmental effects around the monster's location. These often signal the presence of a rare creature.

- **Specific Environmental Conditions:** Rare monsters may only appear during certain in-game conditions, such as at night, in specific weather conditions (rain, thunderstorms), or in certain areas that require you to first unlock or explore hidden zones.

2. How to Track Rare Monsters

Tracking rare monsters involves more than simply wandering through the wilds hoping for a sighting. Here are the steps to effectively track them:

- **Use Monster Tracks and Clues:** As you explore, keep an eye out for tracks, footprints, broken branches, or other environmental clues that indicate a rare monster's presence. These will often lead you in the right direction.

- **Pay Attention to Environmental Signs:** Rare monsters may leave behind distinctive environmental effects. For example, a trail of toxic gas or a shift in the landscape that hints at a monster's path. You might also see certain creatures behaving differently, such as fleeing in terror, indicating that a rare monster is nearby.

- **Listen for Audio Cues:** Sound plays a significant role in tracking rare monsters. Their roars or growls will often sound different from regular monsters and may serve as a directional cue to pinpoint their location.

- **Use the Hunter's Compass and Scout Flare:** Your in-game tools, like the Hunter's Compass, can be an invaluable asset in tracking down rare monsters. Additionally, using Scout Flare items in key locations may reveal their general vicinity, making it easier to locate them.

3. Preparing for the Hunt

Once you've tracked down the rare monster, preparation is key to ensuring your success in the fight. Rare monsters often come with tougher defenses and unique attack patterns, so equipping yourself properly will be essential:

- **Bring the Right Gear:** Ensure that your weapons and armor are upgraded to match the rarity and difficulty of the monster. Many rare monsters will have elemental or status effects that you can exploit, so prepare weapons that counter these weaknesses. For example, if the monster uses poison, bring antidote items or equip armor that protects you from toxic effects.

- **Stock Up on Specialized Items:** Certain rare monsters may have specific weaknesses to particular traps or environmental objects. Bring items like flash bombs, shock traps, or poison-coated ammo that can provide a significant advantage during the battle. Remember that having healing items or a steady supply of buffs will be critical for surviving longer, tougher hunts.

- **Team Composition:** Rare monsters often require careful coordination, especially in co-op play. Make sure that your team is equipped with a variety of weapons that can both support and deal damage. A well-balanced party will improve your chances of survival and success. Ensure that someone on the team is designated as a support role with healing items, traps, and buffs.

4. Battle Strategies for Rare Monsters

Fighting rare monsters is no walk in the park. These creatures are often designed to test the limits of your hunting skills. To increase your chances of success, adopt the following strategies during the fight:

- **Know the Monster's Weaknesses:** Every rare monster has specific weak points, whether it's a body part or elemental vulnerability. Study its behavior carefully, target weak spots (such as the head or tail), and use the appropriate elemental weapons to maximize damage output. Take time to learn when it's most vulnerable such as after a heavy attack or when it's stunned by a trap.

- **Master Dodging and Parrying:** Many rare monsters will unleash powerful, sweeping attacks that can easily knock you out if you're not careful. Master the timing for dodging and parrying to avoid taking unnecessary damage. Be especially alert when the monster is enraged, as its attacks will be more frequent and harder to avoid.

- **Use Traps and Environmental Hazards:** Rare monsters often have a lot of health and can deal devastating blows, so controlling the battlefield is essential. Traps can temporarily immobilize the monster and give you and your team time to regroup or deal extra damage. Also, use the environment to your advantage many areas in *Monster Hunter Wilds* have environmental hazards, such as cliffs or unstable terrain, that can be used to damage the monster or create an opening.

- **Stay Patient and Consistent:** Rare monsters can be drawn-out, intense battles, requiring you to be patient and focus on consistent damage output. If you're not careful, it's easy to make the mistake of over-committing to aggressive tactics and exhausting your resources. Instead, stay focused, watch for openings, and make sure to adapt to the monster's evolving behavior.

4.3 ELEMENTAL STRENGTHS AND WEAKNESSES EXPLAINED

In *Monster Hunter Wilds*, understanding the elemental strengths and weaknesses of both your weapons and the monsters you face is a crucial part of your strategy. Elements can dramatically affect the outcome of a hunt, and knowing how to exploit these vulnerabilities can make the difference between victory and defeat. This section will delve into the different elemental attributes found in the game and how they interact with the various monsters you'll encounter, helping you to tailor your approach for maximum effectiveness.

1. The Six Main Elements and Their Effects

There are six primary elemental attributes that play a vital role in the world of *Monster Hunter Wilds*: Fire, Water, Thunder, Ice, Dragon, and Poison. Each of these elements has its own set of strengths and weaknesses when it comes to weapons, armor, and the monsters you hunt.

- **Fire:** Fire weapons are highly effective against monsters that are weak to heat, such as those from volcanic or desert regions. However, it's less effective against aquatic creatures or those with a natural affinity for the cold.

- **Water:** Water-based weapons are great for combating fire-based monsters or those found in hot, dry climates. Water is also particularly effective against some plant-based monsters, as it can extinguish their fiery traits.

- **Thunder:** Thunder weapons are often used to deal with monsters that have a natural affinity for the earth or rock, such as those that live in caves or underground. Thunder is also effective against flying or airborne monsters, causing them to become stunned or knocked down.

- **Ice:** Ice weapons have a high advantage over fire-based monsters, as they can freeze them in place, dealing massive damage over time. Ice is also good against creatures that are naturally resistant to other elements, making it an effective all-around option for certain hunts.

- **Dragon:** Dragon weapons deal elemental damage that is effective against the toughest monsters, especially elder dragons. These creatures often have unpredictable behavior and extraordinary power, so using Dragon weapons can help weaken their natural defenses.

- **Poison:** Poison-based weapons are useful for chipping away at a monster's health over time, especially against those that don't have a strong resistance to toxic effects. Poison is particularly good against large, slow-moving monsters, as they are harder to dodge when affected by poison damage.

2. Identifying Elemental Weaknesses in Monsters

Each monster in *Monster Hunter Wilds* has its own set of elemental weaknesses. Knowing how to exploit these vulnerabilities will significantly increase your chances of success in battle. Here are some general tips for identifying and exploiting elemental weaknesses:

- **Study Monster Behavior:** Pay attention to the visual cues and behavior of the monster you are hunting. Some monsters will show signs of being weak to certain elements, such as visibly shuddering when hit with an elemental attack or changing color to indicate a vulnerable state.

- **Monster-Specific Elemental Profiles:** Every monster in *Monster Hunter Wilds* has a unique elemental profile. For example, a monster that thrives in a fiery environment might have a strong resistance to Fire, making Water or Ice a better option for exploiting its weaknesses.

- **Research Monster Lore:** When in doubt, check the game's lore or monster entry information to gain insight into a creature's elemental vulnerabilities. Certain monsters are well-known for their weaknesses to specific elements, such as the Dragon-elemental creatures being particularly weak to Ice or Thunder-based attacks.

- **Use Elemental Tools and Buffs:** When facing a monster with known elemental weaknesses, consider using elemental coatings or buffs to enhance your damage output. Coating your arrows with elemental damage or applying elemental powders can make a huge difference in these hunts.

3. Combining Elements for Maximum Damage

While certain weapons are best suited for one particular element, there's an opportunity to combine different elements to increase your effectiveness during the hunt. Here's how you can use elemental combinations for a strategic advantage:

- **Switching Between Elemental Weapons:** If you're playing with a team or in multiplayer, each member can equip a weapon that targets different elemental weaknesses, allowing for a balanced approach. For example, one hunter can use Fire weapons while another uses Water, ensuring that you're prepared for any monster encounter.

- **Elemental Status Effects:** In addition to direct damage, elemental attacks can often trigger status effects that are incredibly useful in battle. For instance, Thunder can paralyze enemies, Ice can freeze them, and Poison can inflict damage over time. Learning when to trigger these effects can give you a massive edge in the fight.

- **Environmental Elemental Traps:** Some areas in *Monster Hunter Wilds* have environmental traps or hazards that can exploit elemental weaknesses. For example, certain traps might be infused with electricity, which can shock and stun monsters weak to Thunder. Knowing when and where to place traps can give you the upper hand.

- **Elemental Affinity Armor and Skills:** Many pieces of armor and skill sets allow you to augment your elemental affinity, increasing the damage you deal with specific elements or reducing the damage you take from them. Investing in armor and skills that align with your preferred element can further boost your performance during hunts.

4. Using Elemental Strategies in Battle

Once you know the elemental strengths and weaknesses of your target, the next step is to implement a strategic approach during the battle itself. Here are some ways to make the most of your elemental knowledge:

- **Target Vulnerable Body Parts:** Many monsters have specific body parts that are particularly weak to certain elements. For example, targeting a monster's wings with Thunder-based weapons might cause it to stagger or fall to the ground, opening it up for additional damage. Aim for weak spots such as heads, tails, or limbs to maximize elemental effects.

- **Adjust Your Tactics During Battle:** Pay attention to your monster's behavior and adapt your tactics accordingly. If you notice that your elemental attacks are having less impact as the monster becomes enraged, switch to a different elemental weapon to continue dealing significant damage.

- **Cooperate with Team Members:** In multiplayer, coordinating elemental attacks with your teammates is key. For example, one player could use Fire attacks to weaken a monster, while another player finishes it off with Water or Ice attacks to capitalize on its elemental vulnerability. This teamwork maximizes efficiency and reduces the time spent in battle.

- **Adapt to Changing Conditions:** Some rare monsters can change their elemental properties during battle, either due to their environment or through special attacks. For instance, a monster might absorb fire energy, making it temporarily resistant to Fire but weak to Ice. Be prepared to adapt quickly by switching weapons or changing strategies when these changes occur.

4.4 CAPTURING VS. SLAYING: WHICH IS BETTER?

In *Monster Hunter Wilds*, hunters are faced with the choice between capturing or slaying monsters. While both options lead to rewards, the decision of whether to capture or slay depends on various factors, including the monster, your goals, and the desired materials. This section will break down the benefits and strategies of both methods to help you decide when to capture and when to slay.

1. The Benefits of Capturing Monsters

Capturing a monster is often seen as a more tactical approach. Instead of slaying the creature, hunters can use specialized traps and tranquilizing items to capture it alive. Here are the key benefits of capturing:

- **Access to Rare Materials:** Capturing monsters is the only way to guarantee certain rare materials that are essential for crafting high-level weapons and armor. Items like monster parts, gems, and certain crafting materials are more likely to drop from a captured monster than one that is slain. This can significantly expedite your gear progression.

- **Faster Hunts and Lower Risk:** Capturing a monster can often be quicker than slaying it, especially if the monster is evasive or has powerful attacks. If you've already dealt enough damage to the monster and it begins to flee or enter a weakened state, capturing it might be a safer and faster route compared to finishing off a slayer battle.

- **Achieving Capture-Specific Rewards:** Certain quests and achievements in *Monster Hunter Wilds* require capturing monsters. Completing these tasks will net you unique rewards, including special items, special equipment upgrades, and even new abilities that can help you during future hunts.

- **More Rewards from Multi-Hunts:** If you are on a quest where you need to capture multiple monsters, doing so can provide additional rewards, such as bonus materials or the opportunity to harvest more items from the same creature. This makes capturing a more rewarding strategy in these specific scenarios.

2. The Benefits of Slaying Monsters

Slaying a monster, on the other hand, offers different advantages, especially in terms of battle satisfaction and overall rewards. Here are the main benefits of slaying:

- **Faster Material Collection for Specific Items:** Some monsters yield the most sought-after materials only when slain. Certain rare materials, such as horns, hides, or claws, are more likely to drop when a monster is killed, especially if you break specific parts during the fight. If you need those materials to upgrade or craft a particular item, slaying might be your better option.

- **Satisfaction and Progression:** There's a certain satisfaction in taking down a monster to its final breath. For many players, the thrill of defeating a monster in combat and the rewards associated with the kill provide a sense of accomplishment. If you're looking for a more intense and action-packed experience, slaying is likely to be the more rewarding path.

- **Targeting Specific Weaknesses:** When you slay a monster, you often have more flexibility in how you approach the hunt. You can focus on exploiting weaknesses, using advanced tactics like traps and combos, or breaking specific parts of the monster to earn extra rewards. Slaying can allow for a more strategic approach, as you have control over when the monster dies.

- **More Hunting Experience:** For players who enjoy the challenge and thrill of combat, slaying monsters provides more experience in handling difficult creatures. The longer, more intense fights often improve your understanding of monster behavior and combat mechanics, making you a better hunter in the long run.

3. Which Method Should You Choose?

The choice between capturing and slaying ultimately comes down to your objectives and playstyle. Here's when you should consider each option:

- **Capture When:**
  - You need rare materials for crafting or upgrading gear.
  - You're focused on completing specific quests or achievements related to capturing monsters.
  - You're after a quicker, safer hunt with less risk of failure.
  - You're playing with a team and want to maximize the rewards for everyone involved.
- **Slay When:**
  - You need certain monster parts that are more easily obtained from slain monsters.
  - You want the thrill of a longer, more intense battle.
  - You're looking to break specific parts of a monster for additional rewards.
  - You want to test your skills against the full might of a creature in combat.
  - You're aiming for higher experience and monster-specific drops.

4. Combining Both Strategies

In *Monster Hunter Wilds*, it's possible to incorporate both capturing and slaying into your hunting routine. Depending on the situation, you may want to capture a monster for the materials and rewards, or slay it for the loot and challenge. Here's how you can strategically use both methods:

- **Capture After Slaying:** In some cases, you may slay the monster first to collect the primary rewards and then capture it afterward for additional materials. This dual strategy works best for monsters that can be easily captured once weakened.

- **Cooperative Hunts:** In multiplayer, team members can work together to balance the capture/slay dynamic. Some players can focus on slaying the monster, while others may focus on preparing traps and tranquilizers for the capture. This can maximize the rewards for the entire group and make the hunt more efficient.

- **Post-Battle Analysis:** After each hunt, take a moment to analyze what you need from the monster. If the primary goal is material gathering, opt for a capture. If the goal is progression and battle experience, focus on slaying.

CHAPTER 5: EXPLORATION AND SURVIVAL IN THE WILDS

5.1 NAVIGATING THE OPEN-WORLD ENVIRONMENTS

In *Monster Hunter Wilds*, the thrill of the hunt extends far beyond combat, with vast and unpredictable open-world environments to explore. Whether you're trekking through dense forests, scaling jagged mountain peaks, or navigating lush swamps, your ability to navigate and adapt to these dynamic landscapes will play a key role in your survival. This section will guide you through the exploration of *Monster Hunter Wilds*'s diverse environments, offering strategies, tips, and insights on how to get the most out of each area.

1. The Role of the Environment in Your Hunt

The environments in *Monster Hunter Wilds* are not merely backgrounds but active, integral parts of your hunting experience. Here's how understanding your surroundings can influence your success:

- **Terrain and Obstacles:** Different areas feature terrain that can either hinder or help your progress. Steep cliffs might offer advantageous high ground for attacks, while swamps may slow your movement. It's essential to recognize these aspects of each environment and use them to your advantage.

- **Monster Behavior and Location:** Each region hosts a variety of monsters, and their behavior is directly influenced by their environment. Some creatures prefer to stay hidden in caves or dense foliage, while others may be aggressive in open areas. Understanding the ecosystem and predicting where monsters are likely to appear can make your hunt more efficient.

- **Resources and Materials:** Every environment is rich in unique resources such as herbs, ores, and materials that are essential for crafting. Knowing where to find them can save you time and provide necessary ingredients for creating potions, traps, and even crafting gear.

- **Weather Conditions:** Dynamic weather plays a role in your hunting strategy. For example, heavy rain might obscure your vision and affect certain attacks, while extreme heat could drain your stamina. Pay attention to weather patterns as they can dictate the best time to hunt specific monsters or the tools you might need.

2. Using the Map and Navigation Tools

The game provides a variety of tools and methods to help you navigate the expansive world. Mastering these tools will ensure that you are always prepared, no matter the environment.

- **Interactive Map:** *Monster Hunter Wilds* features a comprehensive map that displays your current location, points of interest, and resource-rich areas. Make sure to study the map before setting out, as it offers vital information, including potential monster locations and fast-travel points.

- **Waypoints and Markers:** Placing custom markers on your map can help you remember important locations, like caves, camp sites, or particular resources. You can even mark monster dens or quest objectives to streamline your hunt.

- **Scoutfly Assistance:** Scoutflies are your companions in the wild, helping you locate monsters and points of interest. Following their glowing trail can lead you to your prey, while also uncovering hidden paths or new resource nodes.

- **Tracking and Clues:** As you explore, keep an eye out for footprints, scratch marks, and other signs left behind by monsters. Tracking is an important skill in the game, and these clues will guide you towards your target, revealing paths and monster weaknesses.

3. Survival Strategies for Harsh Environments

While hunting and exploration are exciting, *Monster Hunter Wilds* presents real challenges that test your survival instincts. Harsh environmental conditions, limited resources, and the threat of hostile creatures make every decision matter. Here's how to survive and thrive in the wilds:

- **Managing Stamina and Resources:** In vast open-world settings, managing your stamina is crucial. Climbing mountains, sprinting across open fields, or dodging an attack can all drain your energy. Keeping an eye on your stamina meter is important, and carrying stamina-restoring items such as rations or wet stones can prevent disastrous situations.

- **Crafting on the Go:** You'll rarely find yourself fully prepared for every scenario, so being able to craft items while exploring is vital. Whether it's healing potions, traps, or hunting tools, make sure you gather resources during your travels to craft as you go. Crafting stations are often scattered across the map, but don't rely on them entirely.

- **Taking Advantage of Shelter and Safe Zones:** Sometimes, you'll need to take a break to regain health, stamina, or resources. Look for safe zones such as campsites or hidden shelters, where you can rest and recover. These areas may also contain cooking stations, where you can prepare meals for buffs.

- **Staying Prepared for Combat:** You never know when a fight will break out. Always carry a well-rounded selection of tools and weapons. Trap components, bombs, and elemental attacks can help you gain an advantage in unexpected skirmishes. Additionally, knowing when to fight and when to retreat will save your life during encounters with especially powerful or aggressive monsters.

4. Environmental Hazards and How to Overcome Them

Not all threats come in the form of monsters. The environments themselves can pose serious challenges that require preparation and strategy to overcome. Here's what to expect in the wilds and how to handle it:

- **Environmental Traps:** Some areas are rigged with natural traps, such as quicksand, rolling boulders, or poisonous plants. Always stay alert and avoid stepping into dangerous zones. Use your Scoutfly or pay attention to visual cues on the ground to avoid triggering these traps.

- **Extreme Weather:** Certain areas are prone to extreme weather conditions that can affect your visibility, stamina, or health. For example, blizzards might slow your movements and obscure enemy vision, while volcanic areas may cause burn damage over time. Equip yourself with the appropriate gear (e.g., fire-resistant armor in volcanic regions) to mitigate these effects.

- **Hostile Flora and Fauna:** Some plants or creatures in the wild can attack or poison you, especially in dense jungles or near water sources. Keep your wits about you when approaching unknown flora, and be ready to use anti-poison antidotes or healing potions when necessary.

- **Environmental Buffs:** While many hazards exist, there are also natural advantages to utilizing the environment. You can trigger environmental hazards, like explosions in volatile regions or herd monsters into traps like quicksand. Learning how to manipulate your environment can give you a strategic edge during combat.

5.2 GATHERING RESOURCES AND CRAFTING ESSENTIALS

In *Monster Hunter Wilds*, gathering resources and crafting the right items are fundamental components of both your survival and success. Every journey into the wilds requires a careful eye for valuable materials, and how you use these resources can make the difference between life and death. This section will guide you through the essential aspects of resource gathering and crafting, ensuring you're always prepared for whatever challenges lie ahead.

1. Identifying and Harvesting Key Resources

The world of *Monster Hunter Wilds* is brimming with natural resources that can be harvested and used to create vital items for your hunts. Understanding where and how to gather these materials will allow you to craft weapons, armor, and consumables that enhance your hunting abilities.

- **Herbs and Plantlife:** From basic healing items to special buffs, plants play a crucial role in crafting. Look for bright-colored herbs that often grow in open fields or forested areas. Some plants can be combined to create more advanced potions, which can restore health or boost your combat performance.

- **Minerals and Ores:** Throughout the game, you'll come across mining nodes scattered across various environments. These nodes yield valuable ores, which can be used to forge or upgrade weapons and armor. Pay close attention to the rock formations around you, especially in mountainous or cave regions.

- **Monster Parts:** Monsters themselves offer some of the most important crafting materials. Whether it's a monster's bones, scales, claws, or even its hide, harvesting parts after a successful hunt is essential. These materials are used to craft and upgrade equipment, allowing you to improve your gear as you face stronger foes.

- **Fishing and Water Resources:** Some rare items can only be gathered from bodies of water. Fishing provides access to rare fishes, herbs, and other essential resources. Make sure to have a fishing rod ready when you find rivers, lakes, or coastal areas.

2. Crafting and Upgrading Weapons and Armor

Crafting is an essential skill in *Monster Hunter Wilds*, as the items you create will determine how well-equipped you are for future hunts. From weapons that suit your playstyle to the armor that will protect you from the elements or enemy attacks, crafting is the foundation for building a strong hunter.

- **Weapon Crafting:** The game features a wide range of weapon types, and each one requires specific materials to craft or upgrade. When you hunt monsters, keep an eye on their drops for special crafting materials that are unique to their species. These materials can enhance weapon strength, elemental attributes, or even unlock new abilities.

- **Armor Sets:** Crafting armor sets is just as important as crafting weapons. Different sets offer unique bonuses and protection, depending on the monster parts used in the crafting process. Some armor may grant extra stamina, improved resistance to elements, or increased damage against specific monsters. To get the best out of your armor, aim to collect a variety of monster parts and experiment with different sets.

- **Upgrades and Enhancements:** Once you've crafted a basic weapon or armor set, it's important to focus on upgrading and enhancing your gear. Upgrading usually requires additional resources, and in some cases, rare materials found only in the wilds or from higher-level monsters. Consider upgrading your gear to keep up with tougher opponents as you progress through the game.

- **Elemental Effects:** Many weapons and armor sets have elemental properties fire, water, ice, thunder, etc. that can be very useful when fighting monsters with specific weaknesses. Crafting elemental-based gear gives you an edge over certain types of monsters, so always keep track of your enemy's elemental vulnerabilities and craft accordingly.

3. Consumables and Field Items for Success

While your weapons and armor are essential, the consumables you craft play a huge role in ensuring you stay alive during tough hunts. From healing potions to traps, the ability to craft the right items at the right time can turn the tide of battle in your favor.

- **Health Potions and Buffs:** Health potions are the most basic form of healing, but as you progress, you'll want to craft stronger potions that restore more health or grant temporary buffs. Crafting your own potions allows you to tailor your stock to your preferred playstyle, whether you want a boost to attack power, defense, or stamina.

- **Traps and Bombs:** Traps are key for capturing monsters, and bombs are invaluable for dealing massive damage in quick bursts. Make sure to gather resources like trap components and explosive materials to craft these essential items. You'll often need traps to capture certain monsters or disable them temporarily to heal and regroup.

- **Ammo for Ranged Weapons:** If you use ranged weapons like bows or crossbows, crafting ammunition is an essential part of your strategy. Keep an eye on resources like gunpowder, ores, and monster parts that can be used to create special ammunition with various effects, such as explosive or elemental-infused arrows.

- **Food and Meals:** In addition to potions, don't forget the importance of food. Crafting meals provides a range of benefits, from improving your stamina to granting temporary buffs to resist environmental damage or elemental effects. Visit the cooking stations scattered around the map to craft meals that complement your hunting needs.

4. Crafting for Special Gear and Unique Items

Beyond basic weapons and armor, *Monster Hunter Wilds* also features special gear and rare items that are crafted from unique resources. These items often require specific monster drops or rare materials that are more difficult to find but provide significant advantages in combat.

- **Legendary Gear:** Some of the best weapons and armor in the game can only be crafted by gathering extremely rare materials from high-level or rare monsters. These materials are often hard to come by and require skill and patience to gather. However, once crafted, legendary gear offers unparalleled power and special abilities.

- **Special Tools:** In addition to weapons and armor, you can craft special tools that can enhance your performance in the wilds. From bug-catching nets to portable healing devices, these tools are often found through exploration or crafted with rare materials. Always check your inventory and craft any tools that might give you an advantage in the field.

- **Monster-specific Gear:** Some monsters drop unique parts that can be used to craft specialized equipment, such as armor sets that grant bonuses against specific elements or monsters. Look out for these rare pieces of gear, as they can offer you significant advantages in hunts.

- **Cosmetic Items:** While not essential for combat, crafting cosmetic items can add a fun and personal touch to your hunter's appearance. Collect materials for new outfits, weapon skins, and other customizations to express your style.

5.3 HIDDEN AREAS, SECRET PASSAGES, AND RARE FINDS

In *Monster Hunter Wilds*, the world is teeming with secrets waiting to be discovered. Whether it's a hidden cave tucked away in a remote corner or a secret path leading to rare resources, exploring these hidden areas can yield valuable rewards and give you an edge over the toughest monsters. In this section, we'll delve into the hidden areas, secret passages, and rare finds that are scattered throughout the wilds. With the right knowledge, you'll unlock powerful items, find treasure troves, and gain access to environments that few hunters ever see.

1. Discovering Hidden Caves and Ancient Ruins

The wilds are rich in mysterious locations, many of which are hidden from the casual observer. One of the most exciting aspects of the game is discovering these secret caves and ancient ruins that hold precious treasures. These areas are often tucked behind waterfalls, deep in forests, or in seemingly inaccessible cliffsides.

- **Waterfall Caves:** Often found behind or beneath waterfalls, these caves are home to rare minerals and monster parts. To access them, look for areas where the water flow isn't obstructed, and investigate nearby rocky outcrops. Sometimes, special tools or abilities are required to break through barriers to reach these hidden gems.

- **Ancient Ruins:** Scattered across the map are remnants of forgotten civilizations. These ruins often house unique artifacts that can be used in crafting powerful gear or upgrading your existing equipment. Be sure to examine walls and pillars for hidden switches or clues that might reveal a secret entrance.

- **Underground Tunnels:** Some of the most valuable resources in the game can be found deep underground. These tunnels, while often difficult to spot, lead to caverns filled with ores, herbs, and other rare crafting materials. Keep an eye out for cracks in the ground or unusual rock formations that might hint at an entrance.

2. Secret Passages and Hidden Routes

The wilds are a labyrinth of intertwined paths, and not all of them are immediately visible. Secret passages can take you to shortcut routes, hidden resource deposits, or provide a tactical advantage in your monster hunts. Mastering the art of finding these passages will elevate your exploration and give you access to areas that many hunters overlook.

- **Camouflaged Paths:** Some areas in the wilds are camouflaged by dense foliage or rocks that blend in with the surroundings. These hidden paths may appear as part of the natural landscape but can lead you to entirely new zones. Look for areas where the ground changes texture or where certain environmental features seem out of place.

- **Hidden Doors and Switches:** Often hidden in plain sight, secret doors or hidden switches can open up entirely new routes or access points. These can be hidden behind large boulders, underneath thick vines, or within thick foliage. Don't be afraid to inspect your surroundings carefully and look for anything that stands out.

- **Rope Bridges and Climbing Areas:** Some secret paths can only be reached by climbing or crossing precarious rope bridges. These routes lead to areas that are difficult to access through traditional paths but offer incredible rewards. Be sure to bring along climbing gear or tools that may help you access these high vantage points.

3. Rare Finds and Special Resources

One of the most thrilling aspects of exploration in *Monster Hunter Wilds* is finding rare resources and materials that are not only hard to come by but can be used to craft exceptional weapons and armor. These rare finds are typically hidden in out-of-the-way places and require both patience and skill to locate.

- **Rare Monster Parts:** Some of the rarest materials can only be found in hidden areas, dropped by elusive monsters that lurk in the most difficult-to-reach spots. These materials can be used to craft weapons with special abilities or upgrade armor to provide unique resistances. Check high-altitude areas, deep caves, or places where only the most seasoned hunters venture.

- **Legendary Ore Deposits:** In the wilds, legendary ores are scattered in very specific locations and often require advanced knowledge of the terrain to uncover. These ores are used to craft some of the strongest weapons and armor in the game. Keep your eyes peeled for any unusual markings or environmental hints that might suggest the presence of these rare resources.

- **Hidden Treasure Chests:** Occasionally, you'll come across treasure chests tucked away in secret corners of the world. These chests contain items that are either valuable for crafting or simply rare enough to be worth a lot of Mira. Pay attention to the environment, and explore areas that seem to be off the beaten path these chests could be hiding exactly what you need.

- **Special Herbs and Materials:** Some of the rarest crafting materials, like special herbs with potent effects or unique monsters with materials that can't be found anywhere else, are located in hidden spots around the map. These materials can help craft consumables that boost your combat abilities or provide long-lasting buffs.

4. Using Special Tools to Access Hidden Areas

Certain tools in *Monster Hunter Wilds* are specifically designed to help you access hidden areas that would otherwise be unreachable. Knowing how and when to use these tools will unlock many secrets and provide you with additional ways to gather resources or ambush enemies.

- **Bombs and Explosives:** Some walls or obstacles in the environment can only be broken down using explosives. These tools can clear debris or break through blocked paths, allowing you access to caves or secret rooms that might otherwise be inaccessible. Stock up on explosives during your exploration to take full advantage of hidden opportunities.

- **Climbing Gear:** In certain parts of the map, climbing is necessary to reach high ledges or hidden caves. Having climbing gear in your inventory will allow you to scale rocky cliffs and reach hidden ledges where valuable resources can be found. Make sure to equip these tools when you plan to venture into mountainous or steep areas.

- **Fishing Rods:** Some rare resources can only be accessed through fishing, particularly in secret or hard-to-reach bodies of water. A well-stocked fishing rod can yield valuable monster parts or crafting materials, especially in hidden locations like caves or high-altitude lakes.

- **Mapping Tools and Items:** In some cases, maps of the world may have areas that are marked with cryptic symbols or hidden routes. Using specialized mapping tools can reveal secret entrances or forgotten zones, making it easier to find the hidden treasures waiting for you in the wilds.

5.4 WEATHER EFFECTS AND HOW THEY IMPACT GAMEPLAY

The dynamic weather system in *Monster Hunter Wilds* adds an extra layer of depth to the gameplay, influencing both the environment and your hunting strategies. Weather conditions are not just cosmetic; they have a tangible effect on your ability to navigate, hunt, and survive in the wilds. Understanding these effects and adapting your playstyle to the changing weather is essential to becoming a successful hunter. This section will explore the various weather effects in the game and how they can impact your gameplay.

1. Types of Weather Conditions and Their Effects

The game features a variety of weather conditions, each with its own set of challenges and advantages. From heavy rain to scorching heat, the weather plays a critical role in how you approach each hunt and exploration.

- **Rain:** Rain can have a significant effect on both visibility and movement speed. In some areas, it can make the terrain slippery, which may hinder your ability to dodge or maneuver around enemies. However, rain also causes certain monsters to become more active, making them easier to track. Additionally, rainwater can sometimes uncover rare materials that are hidden under rocks or foliage.

- **Heat Waves:** High temperatures can drain your stamina much faster, forcing you to manage your resources carefully during combat. Some areas will also have specific heat-resistant monsters that thrive in these environments. Bring along cooling potions or equipment to mitigate the effects of the heat, or risk exhausting yourself faster than your enemies.

- **Snow and Ice:** Snowfall and icy conditions can severely limit your visibility and movement. Slippery surfaces may make it difficult to maintain balance, which can affect your combat effectiveness. In addition, certain monsters adapt to these environments, using the snow to their advantage by setting traps or camouflaging themselves. Equip yourself with warm gear or resistances to prevent freezing and reduce stamina loss.

- **Fog and Mist:** In foggy conditions, your visibility is drastically reduced, which can make tracking monsters more difficult. However, monsters may also struggle to spot you in these conditions, allowing you to approach them more strategically. Use this to your advantage by setting up ambushes or waiting for enemies to approach, but be mindful of your surroundings as you won't always see what's coming.

- **Windstorms:** High winds can knock you off balance and affect your ranged attacks, making it harder to land accurate shots. However, windstorms can also blow away certain obstacles or even reveal hidden passages, adding a new layer of strategy to your exploration. Take advantage of the wind to uncover secret areas or use it to disrupt monsters' attacks during combat.

2. Weather-Dependent Monster Behavior

The weather not only affects the environment but also the behavior of the monsters you hunt. Different weather conditions trigger various responses from the wildlife, and understanding how these creatures behave in specific weather can give you a huge tactical advantage.

- **Rain:** Some monsters become more aggressive when it rains, while others take shelter, making them easier to hunt. Certain creatures, particularly aquatic monsters, become more active in wet conditions, increasing the chances of encountering them. These creatures may also drop unique materials that are only available during rainy weather.

- **Cold Fronts:** Monsters that thrive in freezing temperatures may become more dangerous during snowstorms, as their attacks could freeze your character and slow your movements. On the other hand, fire-based monsters may become weaker or less aggressive in these cold environments, making them more vulnerable to certain attacks.

- **Wind:** Flying monsters, especially those with wingspans that catch the wind, may be more difficult to target during a windstorm. Their speed and maneuverability are greatly enhanced, making ranged attacks harder to land. Alternatively, monsters that rely on stealth may take advantage of the gusts to stay hidden or reposition quickly, making them more difficult to track.

- **Fog and Mist:** In low-visibility conditions, monsters that rely on stealth tactics become far more dangerous, as they can move around unseen and ambush you from any direction. However, this weather also works to your advantage if you're hunting monsters that rely on sight or are easily startled by noise, as they will have a harder time detecting you.

3. Adapting Your Gear to the Weather

Your success in *Monster Hunter Wilds* heavily depends on how well you prepare for the challenges posed by changing weather conditions. Equipping the right gear and consumables before heading out into a mission will help you avoid costly mistakes and increase your chances of success.

- **Weather-Resistant Gear:** Some armors and accessories are designed to protect you from extreme weather. For example, heat-resistant armor is crucial during heat waves to prevent stamina depletion, while cold-resistant gear helps you stay warm and avoid freezing in snowstorms. Always check the weather forecast before heading out and make sure your gear is up to the task.

- **Elemental Shields and Buffs:** In certain conditions, you may need to use elemental shields or potions that grant buffs to your resistance against the elements. Potions that reduce heat or cold damage can be life-saving during particularly harsh weather.

Additionally, specific shields can negate certain weather effects, allowing you to continue hunting without being hindered by environmental factors.

- **Tools for Adaptation:** Special tools, like cooling or warming crystals, can be carried to combat extreme temperatures. These items can help restore your stamina or prevent status effects like freezing or burning. Similarly, windbreakers and other equipment can help stabilize your movement during windstorms, ensuring that you don't lose your footing in combat.

- **Weapon Adjustments:** Certain weapon types perform better in different weather conditions. For example, ranged weapons like bows or guns may be less effective in high winds, so you may want to opt for close-range weapons such as the greatsword or hammer, which are less affected by weather conditions. Understanding the strengths and weaknesses of your weapon selection will allow you to adapt your strategy as needed.

4. Strategic Combat Adjustments Based on Weather

Combat in *Monster Hunter Wilds* requires more than just a good understanding of your weapons and monsters it's also about how well you adapt to the environment. Weather conditions can shift the tides of battle, so it's crucial to adjust your tactics accordingly.

- **Utilizing Weather to Gain Advantage:** In rainy conditions, for instance, you can use the wet terrain to your advantage by setting traps or using water-based attacks to weaken enemies. In windy conditions, try to use ranged attacks sparingly and instead focus on getting close to monsters for melee strikes. Use environmental features, such as wind gusts or rain, to create openings for your attacks.

- **Managing Weather-Driven Status Effects:** Certain weather conditions can inflict debuffs or negative status effects, such as burning in heat or freezing in the snow. Pay attention to your stamina bar and status icons, and be prepared to use items like healing potions or status cures when needed. Never underestimate the impact of weather on your health and performance during a hunt.

- **Adjusting Your Combat Style to Weather Conditions:** The weather can dictate how you should engage with monsters. For instance, in snowy conditions, movement is slower, so consider using heavy, powerful attacks that are less affected by the slippery terrain. On the other hand, during a foggy situation, stealth-based tactics like surprise attacks and traps can be far more effective in catching enemies off guard.

- **Timing Your Attacks:** Weather conditions often influence the timing of your attacks. When rain pours down, monsters may become more agitated and aggressive, so timing your evasions and attacks is critical to avoiding taking unnecessary damage. In windstorms, watch for a moment of calm in between gusts to line up your ranged shots or launch your aerial attacks.

CHAPTER 6: MULTIPLAYER AND CO-OP STRATEGIES

6.1 SETTING UP AND JOINING HUNTS WITH FRIENDS

In *Monster Hunter Wilds*, hunting isn't just a solo endeavor it's a shared experience that's best enjoyed with friends. Multiplayer and co-op hunts offer a unique dynamic, allowing you to take on some of the game's toughest monsters with a team of skilled hunters. Whether you're forming a team with friends or joining random players, the right strategy and preparation can make the difference between a successful hunt and a devastating failure. In this section, we'll explore how to set up and join hunts with friends, ensuring you're fully prepared for the challenges ahead.

1. Creating a Multiplayer Session

The first step to playing with friends is setting up a multiplayer session. The game offers multiple ways to connect with other hunters, making it easy to jump into a co-op hunt. Here's how to create your own session:

- **Private Session:** If you prefer to play exclusively with friends, creating a private session is the way to go. From the main menu, select the 'Multiplayer' option and then choose to create a private session. You can then invite your friends using their in-game IDs or by sending them a direct invite through your console's friend list.

- **Public Session:** If you're feeling more adventurous or want to meet new people, you can create a public session where other players can join freely. Public sessions are great for picking up additional help, but keep in mind that they can lead to unpredictable dynamics, as each player brings their own approach to combat.

- **Password-Protected Sessions:** For an added layer of security and control, you can opt to set a password for your session. This ensures that only players with the correct password can join, making it a good choice if you want to restrict your session to a specific group of friends.

2. Joining Multiplayer Sessions

Once your session is live, the next step is joining a hunt with others. Whether you're a host or a guest, joining a session is quick and easy, and it's important to ensure that everyone is on the same page before heading into the wilds. Here's what to keep in mind when joining a multiplayer session:

- **Invite via Friend List:** If you're joining a friend's session, you can simply accept an invitation sent via your console's friend system. You'll receive a notification when they've created the session, and with a single click, you'll be in the hunt. Make sure to check the game's session code or password if needed.

- **Searching for Open Sessions:** If you're looking for new players or specific hunts, you can search for open multiplayer sessions. You can filter your search by monster type, difficulty level, and other criteria, ensuring you find a session that matches your skill level and interests. This method is great for players looking to join ongoing hunts without having to set up their own session.

- **Session Settings and Communication:** Before joining a session, take note of the settings, including whether the hunt is on normal or hard difficulty, and the specific monster being targeted. Communication is key, so make sure to coordinate with the team using either the in-game voice chat or text chat to discuss strategies and roles during the hunt.

3. Preparing for a Co-op Hunt

Co-op hunts require a different mindset than solo hunts. With multiple players on the field, you need to work together and adapt to the dynamics of a team. Proper preparation is essential to ensure success:

- **Choosing the Right Weapons:** When hunting in a team, make sure to choose weapons that complement your team's composition. For example, a good balance of ranged and melee weapons can give your team the flexibility to handle different situations. Some hunters may specialize in supporting roles, such as healing or buffing, while others focus on dealing damage or tanking.

- **Stocking Up on Supplies:** Co-op hunts usually take longer than solo ones, so make sure to bring enough healing items, buffs, traps, and bombs. Stock up on resources that will help you and your team survive through extended battles. It's also wise to carry extra tools like Flash Pods or Pitfall Traps, which can help immobilize monsters and create openings for the team to attack.

- **Coordinate Your Strategies:** Before diving into a hunt, take a moment to discuss your approach with your teammates. Decide who will take the lead, who will focus on support, and who will deal the most damage. Communication and team coordination are key to tackling tougher monsters that may overwhelm a less organized group.

- **Be Mindful of Monster Behavior:** In multiplayer, it's important to understand how monsters react to multiple players. Some monsters may target specific players more aggressively, while others might become more unpredictable when facing a full team. Keep an eye on the monster's behavior, and adjust your position or role accordingly to avoid being caught off guard.

4. Etiquette and Teamwork in Co-op Hunts

Successful multiplayer hunting in *Monster Hunter Wilds* is built on teamwork, respect, and clear communication. To get the most out of your hunts and ensure that everyone has a positive experience, follow these basic multiplayer etiquette guidelines:

- **Respecting Each Other's Roles:** Every player in a co-op hunt has a specific role, whether it's dealing damage, providing support, or focusing on crowd control. Respect each hunter's chosen role, and avoid stepping on each other's toes. If someone is designated to heal, let them focus on that job without interference. If you're the damage dealer, focus on putting out as much damage as possible.

- **Sharing Resources:** In multiplayer hunts, sharing resources and items can make a significant difference. If one hunter is running low on healing potions, offer them a few extra to help them out. If a teammate is in danger, consider using a healing item on them or setting traps to prevent the monster from chasing them down. Sharing resources fosters team morale and ensures that no one gets left behind.

- **Communication is Key:** Use in-game voice or text chat to keep everyone updated. Whether it's signaling when you need healing, letting teammates know when a monster is about to unleash a special attack, or calling out for help, effective communication makes all the difference. Being clear and concise helps avoid confusion and keeps everyone on the same page.

- **Stay Positive and Supportive:** Co-op hunts can be challenging, especially when dealing with tough monsters or long battles. Stay positive, encourage your teammates, and keep a sense of humor when things don't go as planned. Remember, every hunt is an opportunity to improve and learn from one another. Support your team through the tough moments, and celebrate the victories together.

6.2 TEAM ROLES AND BEST CO-OP TACTICS

Co-op play in *Monster Hunter Wilds* isn't just about hunting together it's about coordinating roles, planning strategies, and executing tactics that complement each other's strengths. Every member of the team has a specific role to play, and understanding how each role contributes to the overall success of the hunt is key. In this section, we'll break down the essential team roles and best co-op tactics that will give your team the upper hand in any battle.

1. The Damage Dealer (DPS)

The damage dealer, or DPS (damage per second) role, is typically the one focused on dishing out as much damage as possible. These hunters are usually equipped with heavy-hitting weapons that allow them to maximize their damage output, such as greatswords, longbows, or dual blades. However, their effectiveness is highly reliant on the support of their teammates.

- **Weapons of Choice:** Greatsword, Longbow, Dual Blades, Charge Blade

- **Role in the Hunt:** The DPS role is all about maximizing damage during windows of opportunity, such as when the monster is stunned or distracted. They must be agile, taking advantage of openings without becoming overzealous and leaving themselves vulnerable to counterattacks.
- **Best Tactics:** Stay mobile and always be aware of the monster's movements. Positioning is key to avoid taking unnecessary damage, while still being able to unleash powerful attacks. In co-op, communication with your teammates is crucial so that they can create openings for you to strike. Consider coordinating your attacks with other DPS roles to stagger powerful moves.

2. The Tank (Crowd Control and Damage Mitigation)

Tanks play a vital role in taking the brunt of the damage. Their primary job is to divert the monster's attention and absorb as much damage as possible while the DPS roles focus on attacking. Tanks often have the best armor and equipment, enabling them to survive longer in combat.

- **Weapons of Choice:** Sword and Shield, Lance, Gunlance, Hammer
- **Role in the Hunt:** Tanks should focus on controlling the battlefield, positioning themselves between the monster and their teammates to absorb attacks. They use defensive tactics like blocking, parrying, or stunning the monster with heavy blows to create openings for other players. While they might not deal the highest damage, they are indispensable for keeping the hunt in control.
- **Best Tactics:** Always stay close to the monster to keep its attention. Utilize your defensive skills to protect your teammates from harm, especially when the monster targets weaker or more vulnerable members. In co-op, work with your support role to ensure that you're constantly being healed and buffed.

3. The Support (Healing and Buffing)

Support players are the lifeline of any co-op team, ensuring that everyone remains healthy and in fighting shape. Whether through healing items, status buffs, or status ailment prevention, the support role is essential for a successful hunt, especially during longer and more intense battles.

- **Weapons of Choice:** Bow, Insect Glaive, Healing Tools, Support Gunlance

- **Role in the Hunt:** The support role should focus on staying behind the front lines, monitoring the health and well-being of teammates. They can heal injured players, offer status buffs, or provide items that counteract negative effects like poison or paralysis. Support players should also be aware of their teammates' stamina and focus on keeping their abilities active.
- **Best Tactics:** Always keep an eye on your teammates' health and status effects, and use your abilities and items proactively. Don't hesitate to place healing items, buffs, or traps in key locations. It's important to stay mobile and keep a safe distance from the monster while managing your team's health and stamina. Communication with the DPS and tank roles is key to ensuring that your healing is targeted where it's needed most.

4. The Specialist (Trap Setter and Elemental Attacks)

While not always a mainstay in every team, the specialist is crucial for certain strategies, particularly when dealing with larger, tougher monsters. These players are focused on creating opportunities for the team by setting traps, using elemental attacks, or causing status ailments that cripple the monster's ability to fight back.

- **Weapons of Choice:** Light Bowgun, Heavy Bowgun, Insect Glaive, Elemental Hammer, Traps
- **Role in the Hunt:** The specialist's role revolves around setting traps, inflicting elemental damage, or applying status effects like paralysis, sleep, or poison to the monster. Traps and status effects are invaluable tools for breaking the monster's defenses and creating openings for the team to land more powerful hits.
- **Best Tactics:** Focus on applying elemental damage and status ailments that exploit the monster's weaknesses. Keep an eye on the monster's behavior and use traps at strategic points to lock it down when it's vulnerable. Coordinate with your team to ensure the trap is triggered at the right time, and avoid wasting resources by setting the trap when the monster is too mobile.

5. Teamwork and Coordination: Best Co-op Tactics

Once each role is understood, the real power of co-op play lies in seamless teamwork and coordination. To ensure your hunts are effective and fun, you need to master the following co-op tactics:

- **Timing is Everything:** Every member of the team should understand when to focus on dealing damage and when to retreat and heal. Timing large attacks, such as S-Crafts or powerful combos, with your teammates' attacks is essential to overwhelming the monster quickly. Waiting for the right opportunity to strike is critical, and this can only be achieved through communication and team synchronization.

- **Focus Fire:** When dealing with larger monsters, having multiple players attacking the same body part can lead to quicker breaks and weaker points being exposed. Focus fire on specific limbs or weak spots, such as a monster's head or tail, to increase your chances of staggering it or breaking a part for extra rewards.

- **Using Environmental Traps:** The environment itself can be used as a weapon. Whether it's boulders hanging from a cliffside or poisonous plants that can cause an explosion, environmental hazards can give your team the upper hand. Utilize these traps when the monster is close to the environment, but be cautious not to trigger them prematurely or when your teammates are in range.

- **Monitor Stamina and Health:** It's important to keep an eye on your teammates' stamina and health bars. If a teammate is out of stamina, they'll be unable to execute their best attacks or defend themselves properly. The support role should keep an eye on these meters and keep everyone topped off with healing items and stamina boosts.

- **Communication is Key:** Whether using voice chat or in-game messages, keeping everyone updated during the hunt is essential. Let your teammates know when you're using an item, calling for a retreat, or when a monster is about to unleash a devastating attack. Simple, clear communication can make all the difference in ensuring everyone is on the same page and contributing effectively to the hunt.

6.3 COMMUNICATION TIPS FOR EFFECTIVE HUNTING PARTIES

In *Monster Hunter Wilds*, communication can be the difference between a successful hunt and a complete disaster. Whether you're hunting alone with AI companions or teaming up with friends online, maintaining clear and effective communication is essential for coordinating actions, reacting to threats, and ensuring everyone is on the same page. In this section, we'll break down some key communication tips that will make your hunting parties more efficient and enjoyable.

1. Use Voice Chat or Quick Chat Commands

One of the easiest and most effective ways to communicate in *Monster Hunter Wilds* is through voice chat or the quick chat system. Voice chat allows for real-time communication, which is crucial for coordinating attacks, healing, or calling out critical moments in the hunt. If voice chat isn't an option, quick chat commands offer pre-set messages to convey important information without needing to type.

- **Voice Chat:** Always ensure that your microphone is clear and that you're speaking concisely. Avoid talking over each other, and make sure everyone can hear crucial updates, such as when a monster is about to perform a deadly move or when a teammate needs help.

- **Quick Chat:** Quick chat options can save time when things get heated. Use them to signal if you're about to use an item, need healing, or if you're engaging in a certain tactic (like trapping or attacking a weak point). These messages can be tailored to your needs, and using them during intense moments ensures that your team stays on track.

2. Call Out Monster Movements and Attacks

During a hunt, monsters can have unpredictable movements and devastating attacks. Calling out these actions helps your team avoid damage and retaliate effectively. Use voice chat or quick chat to warn teammates when a monster is about to perform a devastating attack, such as a tail swipe, charge, or ground slam.

- **Call Out "Incoming Attack" or "Watch Out":** If you see a monster winding up for a powerful move, alert your team by calling out the action. Let them know if the attack is aimed at them or if it's coming in from a particular direction. For example, if you see a monster start to charge, say "Charging!" to give your teammates time to dodge.

- **Announce Targeted Players:** If the monster is targeting a specific player, inform your teammates so they can adjust their positions or help with crowd control. For example, "Tank, get ready!" or "Support, I need healing!"

3. Coordinate Timing for Powerful Attacks and Traps

Coordinating timing is crucial, especially when using powerful abilities or setting traps. By working together to unleash combined attacks or set up traps, you can break monster parts faster and weaken the monster's overall effectiveness. Let your team know when you're about to use a major attack, and align your actions to maximize damage.

- **Announce Special Attacks:** If you're about to use a powerful move, like a Charge Blade's Elemental Burst or a Greatsword's True Charged Slash, let your teammates know so they can either prepare for a follow-up or avoid interfering. You can say something like, "I'm charging up!" or "Wait for my S-Craft!"

- **Trap Coordination:** If you plan to use a trap, make sure your teammates are aware and that they're positioned in a way that will allow them to capitalize on the trap's effects. For instance, "I'm setting a trap! Keep the monster near!" This way, your teammates will know to position themselves around the trap and prevent the monster from escaping.

4. Share Resources and Status Updates

In *Monster Hunter Wilds*, managing your inventory, health, and stamina is essential for survival. Communicate with your team about the status of your resources and keep them informed of your condition. Sharing healing items, traps, or buffs can turn the tide of battle, especially when someone is running low.

- **Announce Low Health or Stamina:** If you're low on health or stamina, let your team know so they can assist. For example, "Low on health, need a heal!" or "Running out of stamina, need backup!" This keeps your teammates aware of your needs and allows them to react accordingly.

- **Sharing Items:** If you have extra healing items or buffs, offer them to your teammates in need. If you're playing with a support player, let them know if you're running low on supplies so they can replenish you. You can say, "I've got healing potions who needs one?" or "I'm running low on traps, anyone have extras?"

5. Establish a Hunt Strategy Before Engaging the Monster

Before starting the hunt, take a moment to discuss the plan with your team. This can be especially helpful when dealing with larger or more challenging monsters. Assign roles, decide on who will target specific body parts, and ensure that everyone knows their responsibilities. A quick strategy session can save time and prevent confusion during the hunt.

- **Assign Roles:** Discuss who will focus on offense (DPS), who will tank the monster's attacks, and who will focus on healing or setting traps. This allows everyone to understand their role in the hunt and ensures that no one is left scrambling to figure out what they should be doing.

- **Set Expectations:** Let your team know if you plan on using traps, if you're focusing on capturing, or if you'll be taking a more aggressive approach to slay the monster. This sets the tone for the hunt and helps everyone stay on track.

6. Stay Calm During Crisis Moments

When things go wrong, it's easy to panic. However, staying calm and communicating clearly under pressure is vital for a successful hunt. If a teammate is down, or the monster is performing a devastating attack, take a deep breath and communicate the next steps.

- **Keep It Clear and Concise:** In the heat of battle, make sure your messages are short, clear, and to the point. For example, "I'll revive you!" or "Stay back, I'm healing!" This helps your team stay focused and prevents confusion during chaotic moments.

- **Support Under Pressure:** When your team is under pressure, make sure you keep your cool and offer encouragement. A calm

"We've got this!" or "Just a little more, we're almost there!" can keep spirits high and prevent frustration from taking over.

6.4 MULTIPLAYER ETIQUETTE: DO'S AND DON'TS

While *Monster Hunter Wilds* is all about teamwork and collaboration, the social dynamics of multiplayer hunts are just as important as mastering combat mechanics. Understanding proper multiplayer etiquette ensures that everyone enjoys the game, minimizes frustrations, and fosters a positive, cooperative atmosphere. In this section, we'll cover essential do's and don'ts when hunting with others.

1. Do Respect Your Teammates' Playstyles

Every hunter approaches the game differently, and it's essential to respect your teammates' preferred playstyles. Whether they're methodical and defensive or aggressive and fast-paced, flexibility and understanding are key to a smooth multiplayer experience.

- **Recognize Different Roles:** Some players prefer to focus on dealing damage, while others may take on tanking, healing, or supporting roles. Always acknowledge and respect these roles, as they are crucial for team success. Avoid trying to take over a role that someone else has already committed to unless discussed beforehand.

- **Adapt to Your Teammates' Strengths:** If one of your teammates is excellent at drawing the monster's attention, allow them to lead the charge. If someone is known for precision attacks, let them handle weak points. Trust your team's abilities and play in harmony.

2. Don't Rush the Hunt

Rushing through a hunt can lead to mistakes, missed opportunities, and a less enjoyable experience for everyone involved. Taking your time to strategize, communicate, and execute your plan efficiently will result in a more satisfying outcome.

- **Take It Slow:** Avoid sprinting through an area just to reach the monster. Take time to gather resources, gather your thoughts, and plan ahead. Every part of the hunt can provide valuable opportunities, so don't overlook the details. Respect the pace of the hunt, especially if your team wants to explore or gather specific materials.

- **Don't Pressure Your Teammates:** Some players may need extra time to get comfortable with the controls or need more time to figure out their strategy. Be patient with your teammates, and avoid rushing them or making them feel pressured to speed up. It's all about working together at a pace that suits the whole team.

3. Do Communicate, But Keep It Positive

Clear and positive communication is one of the cornerstones of multiplayer etiquette. Keep your messages constructive and friendly, especially in high-stress moments. Providing helpful feedback or encouraging words can make all the difference in maintaining a positive team spirit.

- **Provide Constructive Feedback:** If you need to point something out, do so with kindness. For example, instead of saying "You're not doing your job," try "Let's focus on hitting the monster's weak point" or "Can you draw its attention while I heal?" This keeps the atmosphere supportive and allows the team to improve without feeling criticized.

- **Encourage and Praise Your Team:** Everyone appreciates positive reinforcement. Whether it's a successful hunt, a well-executed trap, or a brilliant piece of teamwork, always give credit where it's due. A simple "Nice shot!" or "Great job, team!" can boost morale and foster camaraderie.

4. Don't Be Afraid to Ask for Help

Everyone starts somewhere, and no one expects you to be perfect right away. If you're struggling or unsure about something in the game, don't hesitate to ask for help. A cooperative multiplayer experience is built on mutual support.

- **Ask for Guidance:** If you're new to the game or a specific weapon, ask your teammates for tips or advice. Most players are more than happy to share their knowledge, and asking questions shows that you're willing to learn and grow as a hunter.

- **Don't Be Shy About Needing a Revive:** Sometimes, things go wrong, and you'll find yourself downed during a hunt. Don't be afraid to ask for a revive. In a team-based game, everyone should support each other, and a well-timed revival can turn the tide of a battle.

5. Do Avoid Disrupting the Flow of the Hunt

Disrupting the flow of the hunt can be frustrating for everyone involved. Whether it's excessive afk time, leaving the hunt early, or starting unnecessary side activities, try to maintain a focus on the hunt itself.

- **Stay Engaged:** If you're playing with others, it's important to stay active and focused on the hunt. Don't wander off unnecessarily or stop participating unless absolutely needed. If you need to take a break, communicate with your team first. Likewise, if you're in a group, don't abruptly leave the hunt without explaining why. It's always polite to give your team a heads-up.

- **Avoid Causing Distractions:** Whether it's spamming chat with irrelevant messages or interrupting others' strategies, avoid causing unnecessary distractions. If something important comes up, share it in a concise and clear manner without taking attention away from the main task.

6. Don't Take the Game Too Seriously

At the end of the day, *Monster Hunter Wilds* is a game meant to be fun and enjoyable. While teamwork and strategy are essential for success, remember that not everything will always go according to plan. It's important to keep a sense of humor, stay lighthearted, and not let setbacks derail your experience.

- **Stay Positive During Failures:** Don't let failures or setbacks turn into frustration. Every hunter has had their share of hunts gone wrong. The key is to laugh, learn from mistakes, and try again. Don't take things personally, and avoid arguing with teammates. Instead, focus on how you can improve as a team for the next hunt.

- **Enjoy the Journey:** Remember that *Monster Hunter Wilds* is about exploring, hunting, and improving. Every monster, every hunt, and every battle is an opportunity to grow and enjoy the world. Keep the experience fun, and don't lose sight of why you started playing in the first place.

CHAPTER 7: QUEST AND PROGRESSION GUIDE

7.1 UNDERSTANDING QUEST TYPES AND OBJECTIVES

In *Monster Hunter Wilds*, quests are at the heart of your progression. From simple hunts to epic, multi-layered adventures, quests offer both structure and freedom, giving players the chance to explore, battle, and gather in a variety of ways. Knowing the types of quests you'll encounter and how to approach them is essential for mastering the game. This section will break down the key quest types, their objectives, and how to efficiently navigate them to maximize your gameplay experience.

1. Main Story Quests: Advancing the Plot

Main story quests are the primary driving force behind your adventure in *Monster Hunter Wilds*. These quests are crucial for progressing through the game and unlocking new regions, weapons, and monsters to hunt. As you advance through these quests, you'll encounter pivotal moments in the story, and these quests will guide your overall experience.

- **Storyline Progression:** Completing main quests reveals significant plot details, introduces new characters, and deepens your connection to the world of *Monster Hunter Wilds*. These quests are designed to be more narrative-driven, pushing the boundaries of your understanding of the world and what's at stake.

- **Quest Difficulty:** Main story quests gradually increase in difficulty, requiring you to hone your skills and adapt your strategy. These quests are typically longer, with more complex objectives, including multi-stage battles or the introduction of major bosses.

- **Rewards:** Completing these quests rewards you with new weapons, armor sets, and crucial items that help further your adventure. The main story quests often provide some of the game's best progression rewards, so prioritize them if you want to unlock the full potential of your hunter.

2. Side Quests: Optional Tasks with Valuable Rewards

While main story quests drive the plot forward, side quests are equally important. These optional tasks allow you to explore different aspects of the game that might not be critical to the storyline but provide valuable rewards and enhancements. Side quests help you gather resources, hunt specific monsters, and refine your skills outside the main narrative.

- **Variety of Objectives:** Side quests come in all shapes and sizes, from hunting down particular monster species to collecting specific materials or assisting NPCs in need. These quests often explore different elements of the game's world and provide you with the freedom to tailor your gameplay experience to your preferences.

- **Skill and Resource Building:** Completing side quests helps you improve your character by allowing you to gather items for crafting, upgrading armor, and testing new weapon types. They also provide experience points, which are useful for leveling up your hunter and unlocking new abilities.

- **Hidden Rewards:** Many side quests offer special hidden rewards, such as unique materials, rare crafting items, or even the ability to encounter legendary monsters. Completing them adds depth to your gameplay experience, often unlocking content that's not immediately available in the main storyline.

3. Timed and Limited-Time Quests: Special Challenges with Unique Rewards

Timed and limited-time quests are a unique feature in *Monster Hunter Wilds*. These quests introduce a sense of urgency and excitement by offering special challenges that are only available for a limited period. Completing these quests within the designated time frame rewards you with exclusive rewards, some of which are not available through regular gameplay.

- **Special Time-Limited Events:** These quests often coincide with in-game events or special promotions, offering you the opportunity to hunt rare monsters, gather special materials, or participate in themed hunts. They create a dynamic aspect to the game, keeping the experience fresh and exciting.

- **Limited-Time Rewards:** Timed quests offer exclusive rewards such as skins, special gear, or powerful items that give your hunter a unique edge. These rewards are usually themed after the event and can be extremely valuable for players looking to customize their gameplay experience or obtain hard-to-find resources.

- **Collaboration with Multiplayer:** Many timed quests are designed to be completed in multiplayer mode, making them a fantastic way to build camaraderie with fellow players. These quests may also come with higher difficulty levels, so teamwork is often crucial for success.

4. Guild Quests: Cooperative Missions for Team Play

Guild quests are designed with teamwork in mind, allowing players to group up and tackle challenges together. These quests often involve more difficult hunts and require a group to strategize, communicate, and work cohesively to achieve success.

- **Collaborative Efforts:** Guild quests typically require multiple players to join forces, making them ideal for friends or other players looking for cooperative experiences. These quests often come with challenging objectives, and the team will need to rely on each other to survive and succeed.

- **Increased Difficulty:** Expect guild quests to have higher difficulty levels compared to solo hunts. Monsters may have increased health, more complex attack patterns, or additional mechanics that require careful planning and coordination. Be ready to adapt your strategy depending on the monster you face.

- **Reward System:** Guild quests usually provide significant rewards for the team's efforts, such as rare materials or exclusive gear. The more challenging the quest, the better the potential rewards, which may include upgrades for weapons and armor sets tailored for team play.

5. Gathering Quests: Scavenge and Harvest the Land

While many of your quests will focus on monster hunting, gathering quests are essential for crafting, upgrading, and maintaining your gear. These quests task you with collecting specific materials from the environment or defeating particular monsters for their parts.

- **Resource Collection:** Gathering quests typically ask you to collect herbs, ores, or parts from monsters. These quests are perfect for hunters looking to upgrade their gear or stock up on crafting items. They're ideal for when you want a break from combat but still wish to advance your character.

- **Strategic Gathering:** Some materials are found in remote locations or require specific weather conditions to appear. You may also need to track down elusive monsters whose parts are integral for crafting advanced weapons and armor. The game encourages strategic planning for resource gathering, requiring you to plan ahead.

- **Complementing Other Quests:** Gathering quests are often tied to the completion of other hunts or missions, acting as a supplementary task that rewards you with resources needed for your more significant goals. Completing these quests allows you to craft powerful new items, ensuring you're always prepared for the next challenge.

7.2 BEST SIDE QUESTS FOR RARE REWARDS

Side quests in *Monster Hunter Wilds* aren't just a way to pass the time : they're a fantastic opportunity to unlock rare and valuable rewards. These quests often lead you to hidden gems that will enhance your arsenal, gear, and overall progression. If you're aiming for the best gear, rare crafting materials, or unique items that can't be found in the main storyline, side quests are your best bet. In this section, we'll explore some of the most rewarding and fascinating side quests you'll encounter and how to maximize the rewards you get from them.

1. Legendary Beast Hunts

One of the most exciting and rewarding side quests in *Monster Hunter Wilds* is hunting down legendary beasts that roam the wilds. These creatures are often elusive, powerful, and require advanced hunting techniques to track and defeat.

- **Overview:** These quests task you with hunting rare and formidable monsters that aren't part of the main story. They often come with their own unique mechanics, including rare attacks and behaviors that require you to think strategically.

- **Rare Rewards:** Completing these hunts grants you rare materials, often used for crafting legendary weapons or special armor sets. These items are often a significant step up in power compared to those found from regular monsters.

- **Challenges:** Legendary beasts are challenging and usually require the coordination of several hunters. Ensure you have the right team composition and powerful gear to take them down.

2. Elemental Essence Gatherer

The Elemental Essence Gatherer side quest involves searching for rare elemental resources scattered across the world. Completing this quest rewards you with powerful elemental items that can boost your elemental damage, resistances, or craft potent elemental-based weapons.

- **Overview:** You'll be tasked with gathering rare resources that correspond to different elemental types such as fire, water, ice, or lightning. These materials are scattered across the world, often in dangerous or hard-to-reach areas.

- **Rare Rewards:** The reward for completing this quest is often elemental-infused gear or crafting materials that will enable you to create weapons with strong elemental effects. These weapons can be crucial in dealing with monsters weak to specific elements.

- **Strategic Approach:** This quest often requires you to be observant and explore every corner of the environment to find the right elemental nodes. Keep an eye on the in-game weather and time of day, as certain elements are more abundant during specific conditions.

3. Master Craftsman's Request

The Master Craftsman's Request is a side quest that challenges you to collect specific items needed to craft rare and powerful armor and weapons. These quests often involve gathering parts from hard-to-find monsters or hidden areas and can unlock high-level crafting options.

- **Overview:** This quest asks you to gather rare materials or hunt specific monsters that drop unique crafting items. The reward is usually a special crafting blueprint or the ability to upgrade existing gear to its maximum potential.

- **Rare Rewards:** The best rewards from this quest are the rare blueprints for weapons or armor that are crafted with some of the game's toughest materials. These items can significantly enhance your character's abilities, making you more capable in future hunts.

- **Tips for Success:** To succeed in this quest, make sure you're well-equipped to hunt down the specific monsters required for these materials. Some of the materials may require specific weather or environmental conditions to appear, so preparation and patience are key.

4. The Hidden Temples and Ruins Questline

The Hidden Temples and Ruins questline involves finding ancient, forgotten places in the wilds that hold secrets, treasures, and long-lost technology. These quests are often linked to in-game lore, and completing them rewards you with unique artifacts and gear.

- **Overview:** These side quests usually require you to explore deep into remote regions of the world where ancient ruins or temples are hidden. These areas are often filled with puzzles, traps, and rare enemies guarding the treasures within.

- **Rare Rewards:** Completing the Hidden Temples and Ruins quests unlocks unique artifacts or powerful relics that provide various buffs, stat boosts, or even open the way to crafting some of the rarest items in the game.

- **Special Note:** Some of these quests are time-sensitive or require you to solve riddles within the temples to access the treasure chests. Pay attention to the environment and look for clues that could help you unlock the next part of the puzzle.

5. The Cartographer's Request

The Cartographer's Request involves uncovering uncharted areas on the map by completing specific side quests that require you to explore new and hidden regions. These quests often lead you to areas that contain valuable materials, rare creatures, and hidden treasures.

- **Overview:** This questline encourages exploration and rewards you for discovering new locations. Each new area you uncover could lead to a monster fight, a hidden resource, or a new area to gather rare items.

- **Rare Rewards:** The rewards for these quests often include powerful materials, rare crafting items, and access to secret areas that contain some of the most valuable resources in the game.

- **Exploration Tips:** As you venture into uncharted territories, be prepared for higher-level monsters and more dangerous environments. Take your time to carefully explore and document all the places you visit, as each discovery brings you closer to the ultimate rewards.

7.3 EFFICIENT PROGRESSION STRATEGIES FOR FAST LEVELING

Leveling up quickly in *Monster Hunter Wilds* requires a mix of smart hunting, resource management, and strategic planning. Progression is not only about defeating monsters but also optimizing your approach to quests, gathering resources, and crafting powerful gear. Whether you're a new hunter or a seasoned veteran looking to accelerate your leveling process, this section will outline the best strategies for maximizing your XP and quickly climbing the ranks.

1. Focus on High-Reward Hunts

Not all monsters are created equal, and focusing on high-reward hunts will ensure you gain the most experience points per unit of effort. Look for monsters that yield significant experience rewards, rare materials, or are part of quests with increased XP payouts.

- **Choose Monster Hunts Wisely:** Prioritize high-level monsters that offer the most experience points, but be mindful of their difficulty. Hunting larger, more dangerous creatures often yields better rewards, but it's important to know when you're ready to face them.

- **Take Advantage of Event Quests:** Event quests or special hunting events are a fantastic way to gain a substantial amount of XP in a short period. These quests often feature monsters with boosted experience rewards or offer multiple high-level monsters to hunt in a single mission.

- **Group Hunts for More XP:** If possible, team up with other players to tackle tough monsters. While the difficulty will increase, so will the reward. Defeating a challenging foe with a team will grant you a substantial amount of experience compared to a solo hunt.

2. Master the Art of Quest Efficiency

Efficient questing is key to fast leveling. The more quests you can complete in a short amount of time, the faster you'll progress. Some quests are designed for speed, while others allow you to gain multiple rewards from a single activity.

- **Stack Quests:** Whenever possible, take on multiple quests that overlap in objectives. For example, if you're hunting a monster that drops valuable crafting materials, check if there are other quests that require the same materials or the same monster, so you're completing more than one task at once.

- **Focus on Completionist Quests:** Certain side quests, particularly ones that involve completing objectives across multiple hunts or missions, offer a large boost to your XP. These can be a bit more time-consuming but can lead to major progression boosts if done consistently.

- **Use Quest Bonuses:** Some quests come with bonus XP for completing secondary objectives or specific conditions (e.g., completing a quest in under a certain amount of time or defeating a monster using specific techniques). Make sure to always check these bonuses to maximize your rewards.

3. Maximize Resource Gathering and Crafting

Gathering and crafting may seem like a side activity, but in *Monster Hunter Wilds*, it's an essential part of the leveling process. Crafting new weapons and armor or upgrading your existing gear ensures you're always prepared for tougher hunts, and resource gathering helps you level up your crafting abilities.

- **Gather Resources Efficiently:** Focus on gathering resources as you hunt, especially those that are required for crafting new gear or upgrading your existing armor and weapons. Some resources provide large XP bonuses when used in crafting recipes, so always make sure to pick up anything that could potentially help you level up.

- **Craft and Upgrade Regularly:** Don't just focus on leveling up your hunter's combat skills. Regularly upgrading your weapons and armor ensures you're always equipped for harder quests. Crafting new items from rare materials rewards you with experience and gives you a much-needed edge in combat.

- **Capitalize on Loot Drops:** Pay attention to any loot drops that come from monsters or environmental interactions, especially those with higher XP value. Many of these resources can be used to craft better gear, which in turn boosts your progression.

4. Combat Training: Focus on Efficiency and Precision

Combat is central to leveling up in *Monster Hunter Wilds*. The more efficient and precise your combat strategies are, the quicker you'll be able to take down monsters, earning more XP in the process. Here's how to improve your combat efficiency:

- **Perfect Your Hunting Techniques:** Focus on mastering a select few weapons or combat techniques that suit your playstyle. By honing your skills, you'll be able to defeat enemies more efficiently, which means fewer resources used per hunt and more XP gained per mission.

- **Use Elemental Weaknesses to Your Advantage:** Understanding monster weaknesses and exploiting them with elemental weapons or attacks is crucial for quicker hunts. Monsters with elemental vulnerabilities can be dispatched faster, leading to more XP in a shorter amount of time.

- **Play Smart in Battles:** Avoid wasting time on unnecessary attacks and focus on optimal moves. Using dodges, parries, and well-timed attacks will help you minimize the duration of hunts, allowing you to maximize the number of hunts you can complete in a given time.

5. Focus on Teamwork and Multiplayer Hunts

While solo play can be rewarding, multiplayer hunts offer a whole new set of advantages. Teaming up with others not only allows you to take on stronger monsters but also speeds up your hunts, maximizing your XP gain per hunt.

- **Team Up for Harder Hunts:** In multiplayer, you can tackle more difficult monsters and quests that would take much longer to complete solo. Each team member brings their own set of skills and weapons, which can help you defeat tougher monsters quicker and more efficiently.

- **Divide and Conquer:** When hunting with a team, each member can specialize in a certain role, such as tanking, dealing damage, or supporting. Having clearly defined roles ensures that each hunt is as efficient as possible, meaning you'll get more XP for less effort.

- **Play with Friends or Co-op Partners:** Multiplayer with friends or co-op partners is the most enjoyable and rewarding way to gain experience. Working with people you know can lead to a faster and more strategic approach to hunting, which helps you level up faster.

7.4 EVENT QUESTS AND LIMITED-TIME CHALLENGES

Event quests and limited-time challenges in *Monster Hunter Wilds* offer some of the most rewarding and exciting opportunities for hunters looking to level up quickly and gain exclusive rewards. These quests are typically time-sensitive and are often tied to in-game events or updates, bringing unique monsters, rare materials, and special rewards that can significantly enhance your progression. In this section, we'll explore how to make the most out of these special quests and challenges, ensuring you don't miss out on valuable loot and experience.

1. Participating in Event Quests

Event quests are special missions introduced periodically throughout *Monster Hunter Wilds*. These quests often feature rare monsters, special environmental conditions, or additional objectives that are not found in the regular story missions. Event quests are a great way to acquire rare materials, upgrade gear, and gain bonus experience points.

- **Check for Active Events Regularly:** Event quests are often tied to real-world events or updates within the game. To stay ahead of the curve, check the in-game bulletin board or community announcements for information on upcoming or active event quests.

- **Focus on Quest Rewards:** Event quests often feature exclusive materials or high-tier rewards that cannot be found anywhere else. Make sure to complete these quests to obtain unique crafting materials, weapons, armor, or even cosmetic items.

- **Limited-Time Event Quests:** These quests are typically available for a short period, so it's crucial to participate in them as soon as they are introduced. Missing an event quest means missing out on valuable rewards, so plan accordingly to maximize your chances of completing these missions.

2. Maximizing Event Rewards

Event quests often offer additional rewards on top of what's normally available in the game. This could include rare monster drops, event-specific currencies, or special gear that gives you an edge in future hunts. Here's how you can maximize the benefits of participating in event quests:

- **Complete Event Objectives:** Many event quests come with specific challenges or objectives that grant extra rewards upon completion. These objectives may include defeating a monster within a time limit, using a particular weapon type, or defeating multiple monsters in a single quest. Completing these objectives will reward you with bonus experience points and materials.

- **Farm Rare Event Materials:** Certain event quests will allow you to farm materials or weapons that are exclusive to that quest. Take advantage of these opportunities to upgrade your arsenal with unique or powerful gear that can help in future hunts.

- **Save Event Currency for High-Tier Rewards:** Some events offer special currency or tokens that can be spent on exclusive rewards, such as limited-edition armor or rare items. Be sure to save these for high-tier rewards that are hard to come by during regular gameplay.

3. Limited-Time Challenges and Their Rewards

Limited-time challenges are often released alongside event quests and provide even more opportunities to earn experience points and exclusive items. These challenges may require you to complete specific objectives, such as defeating a set number of monsters, crafting certain items, or collecting rare materials within a given time frame. Here's how to make the most out of these time-sensitive challenges:

- **Prioritize Challenge Goals:** Limited-time challenges usually have specific goals that can be tracked in the quest log. Focus on completing these challenges efficiently by selecting quests that align with the challenge objectives. This will allow you to earn additional rewards without having to go out of your way.

- **Participate in Global Challenges:** Occasionally, the game will feature global challenges where players around the world work together to achieve specific milestones, such as defeating a certain number of monsters. These challenges often offer generous rewards and can be an excellent way to earn exclusive in-game currency or powerful gear.

- **Optimize Your Playtime for Limited Challenges:** Time-limited challenges ca be overwhelming if you try to tackle them all at once.

Plan your sessions to maximize the time spent on completing the most rewarding objectives, ensuring that you're making the most of your limited playtime.

4. How to Keep Track of Event and Challenge Schedules

To fully benefit from event quests and limited-time challenges, you'll need to stay on top of the game's release schedule. Keeping track of when these events are happening will allow you to plan your hunting sessions and maximize your rewards.

- **Stay Updated on Patch Notes:** Developers regularly release patch notes and announcements detailing upcoming events and challenges. Keep an eye on the game's website or social media channels to stay updated on what's coming up next.

- **Join Community Groups:** Many *Monster Hunter Wilds* communities, including forums, Discord channels, and social media groups, share information on upcoming events and challenges. Joining these communities can provide you with tips on the best strategies to approach these time-limited quests.

- **Set Reminders for Limited-Time Events:** With event quests and challenges being time-sensitive, it's easy to forget about them if you're not careful. Set reminders or mark your calendar for upcoming events so you never miss an opportunity to participate in them.

CHAPTER 8: ECONOMY, CRAFTING, AND RESOURCE MANAGEMENT

8.1 BEST WAYS TO EARN ZENNY FAST

In *Monster Hunter Wilds*, Zenny (the game's primary currency) is essential for upgrading your gear, purchasing items, and unlocking various in-game services. Earning Zenny efficiently is key to making rapid progress in the game, especially as you advance and begin facing tougher monsters. In this section, we'll explore some of the most effective strategies for earning Zenny quickly and reliably, ensuring you always have the resources you need for your next big hunt.

1. Prioritize High-Reward Hunts

The most straightforward way to earn Zenny in *Monster Hunter Wilds* is by completing hunts, but not all hunts are created equal when it comes to Zenny rewards. Some monsters drop a greater quantity of Zenny or materials that can be sold for large amounts of money. To maximize your Zenny earnings, focus on hunting monsters that give higher payouts.

- **Choose Target Monsters Wisely:** Some monsters, such as larger or rarer species, will reward you with more Zenny upon defeat. These hunts can take longer, but the rewards are usually worth the effort, especially when you sell the materials obtained from their carcasses.

- **Target Monsters with Valuable Parts:** As you hunt, make sure to focus on obtaining rare materials and parts that can be sold for a higher value. Parts like scales, claws, or specific monster drops can often be sold to vendors for significant amounts of Zenny, even more so if you have multiple items to sell at once.

2. Sell Unwanted Materials

As you venture through the Wilds, you will accumulate a large number of materials, some of which may not be immediately useful for your gear crafting or progression. While some of these materials are required for specific items or upgrades, others can be sold for extra cash. Be sure to keep a constant eye on your inventory and sell off items you don't need to boost your Zenny reserves.

- **Crafting Materials for Sale:** Certain common materials, like herbs or mining ores, might not have immediate use in your current crafting plans. These can be sold to vendors for a fair amount of Zenny and can free up space in your inventory for more important items.

- **Sell Excess Monster Parts:** When you defeat monsters, you'll gather an array of materials that may not be needed for your gear crafting. Instead of holding onto these items, consider selling them for quick Zenny. However, be cautious not to sell anything essential for your crafting goals.

3. Participate in Trading and Market Exchanges

As you advance through the game, you will have access to trading opportunities. These opportunities allow you to exchange surplus items or resources for a significant amount of Zenny, depending on the rarity of what you're trading. This method is incredibly efficient if you've been hunting specific monsters that drop valuable items.

- **Use the Trading System:** Many in-game vendors will accept rare materials or monster parts in exchange for Zenny. Sometimes, they may offer you more Zenny for certain items that are in high demand at that particular moment, so be sure to check back with vendors often to see if their offers change.

- **Check the Market Regularly:** Some areas of the game will feature dynamic marketplaces where you can sell your materials for a better price. If you have a surplus of rare resources, try to get the best return by taking advantage of market fluctuations and trading opportunities.

4. Focus on Gathering Resources While Hunting

A highly effective way to accumulate Zenny during hunts is by actively gathering resources throughout your journey. These resources can often be sold to vendors, or they can be used to craft items that sell for high amounts of Zenny when completed. Making resource collection a part of your regular hunting strategy will allow you to passively build your Zenny reserves while you focus on the action.

- **Gathering While Exploring:** While hunting monsters, don't forget to harvest resources from the environment. Look for plants, mushrooms, ores, and other materials scattered throughout the world. These resources can be sold directly to vendors or used in crafting to create high-demand consumables and gear upgrades.

- **Be Efficient with Time and Movement:** Gather resources during your hunts without taking too much time away from the main mission. Aim to gather key items as you pass through certain areas, making the most out of every hunting session without it slowing down your overall pace.

5. Complete Bounties and Special Contracts

Throughout your journey, you'll be given bounties and special contracts that reward you with Zenny and other valuable materials for completing specific tasks. These tasks often require you to hunt certain monsters or gather specific resources. By actively seeking out and completing these bounties, you'll not only make progress in your quests but also earn a substantial amount of Zenny.

- **Complete All Bounties:** Make it a habit to check the bulletin boards in the game for new bounties. These tasks usually provide significant Zenny rewards, and some of them might even unlock rare materials that are worth much more when sold.

- **Tackle Special Contracts:** Special contracts often reward you with Zenny for completing more challenging objectives. These can include hunting larger or more powerful monsters, crafting specific items, or participating in timed challenges. Take on these contracts for an added bonus to your Zenny pool.

6. Utilize Daily and Weekly Challenges

To keep players engaged, *Monster Hunter Wilds* offers daily and weekly challenges that reward you with Zenny, items, and experience points for completing specific tasks. These challenges are designed to encourage players to return regularly and take on smaller, bite-sized objectives that reward consistent play.

- **Log in for Daily Rewards:** Make sure to log in daily to claim your free rewards. Completing the daily tasks or challenges might seem small, but over time, these rewards will add up to a substantial amount of Zenny, providing you with extra funds for your gear upgrades.

- **Stay on Top of Weekly Objectives:** Weekly challenges typically involve more substantial tasks, such as completing certain hunts or gathering specific items. Tackling these objectives will not only net you Zenny but will also help you progress faster through the game's progression system.

8.2 TRADING, BARTERING, AND BUYING RARE ITEMS

In *Monster Hunter Wilds*, the ability to trade, barter, and purchase rare items is vital for progressing in the game. As you hunt and explore the vast world, you'll come across many resources, items, and rare materials that can be exchanged for significant rewards. Whether you're looking to upgrade your gear, acquire powerful weapons, or stock up on useful items, knowing how to navigate the game's trading and bartering system will enhance your overall experience.

This section delves into the best strategies for trading, bartering, and buying rare items, ensuring you get the most value out of your hard-earned resources and Zenny.

1. Understanding the Barter System

Bartering plays a significant role in *Monster Hunter Wilds*, offering a way for players to exchange items without using Zenny. This system can be highly rewarding, especially when you are in need of rare materials, crafting components, or specialized gear. However, knowing how to maximize the value of your trades is key to making the most of this system.

- **How to Trade Materials for Rare Items:** Often, the game will allow you to barter your monster parts or rare resources in exchange for powerful items, special armor upgrades, or rare crafting components. These exchanges can be a more efficient use of resources, as some items can be far more valuable than their

Zenny equivalent.

- **Bartering with Vendors and NPCs:** Throughout the world, various NPCs and vendors will offer bartering opportunities. These merchants might offer you rare and valuable items, such as rare ores, potions, or even unique armor, in exchange for specific materials you can gather from defeated monsters. Keep track of their requests and try to fulfill them for a significant return.

- **How to Get the Best Deals:** To ensure you're getting the most from bartering, pay attention to the market's fluctuating demands. Some materials are in higher demand than others at different points in the game, so timing your trades right can net you a better deal. Also, always compare the offers across different vendors, as some may offer better items or lower trade costs than others.

2. Trading with Fellow Hunters

Beyond in-game NPCs, *Monster Hunter Wilds* also allows you to trade directly with other players, creating a dynamic and player-driven economy. Trading with fellow hunters opens up opportunities to acquire items that you may not be able to obtain through standard hunting or crafting.

- **What to Offer and What to Look for:** When trading with other players, it's essential to understand the value of your own items. Some items, such as monster parts or rare materials, are highly sought after by other hunters and can be exchanged for something equally valuable. Offering useful materials for specific upgrades or high-tier items can be a great way to expand your gear quickly.

- **Using Online Trading Systems:** As you progress, you'll gain access to online trading systems where you can list your own items for trade. Always keep an eye on the active trades to see if there are items you need at reasonable prices. This system can help you build up your inventory with rare items that you might struggle to find on your own.

- **Building Relationships with Other Players:** Establishing relationships with fellow hunters can lead to more favorable trades. Trustworthy trading partners may offer you better deals in the future, especially when you engage in consistent exchanges.

Make sure to return the favor to create a mutually beneficial relationship.

3. Purchasing Rare Items from Vendors

While trading and bartering are essential, the ability to purchase rare items directly from vendors remains one of the most reliable ways to acquire powerful gear and upgrades. Many of the game's merchants offer specialized items that are either difficult to find in the wild or can be expensive in terms of the amount of time you need to invest to gather them.

- **Where to Find Rare Vendors:** Throughout the game world, you'll encounter various vendors who specialize in selling rare and exclusive items. Some of these merchants can only be found in specific regions or after reaching certain milestones in the game, while others are available for a limited time during special events.

- **How to Use Zenny Efficiently:** When purchasing rare items, it's important to plan your Zenny spending. Prioritize purchases that offer long-term benefits, such as weapons or armor that provide substantial stat boosts or special effects. Save your Zenny for these important investments, and avoid spending it on consumables or items that can be easily obtained elsewhere.

- **Limited-Time Offers and Discounts:** Certain vendors will offer rare items during special events or time-limited sales. Make sure to check in with vendors regularly, as you may encounter limited-time offers that can significantly improve your hunting potential. These rare items often come with high price tags, but they can provide a major advantage in the early or mid-game.

4. Special Trading Opportunities in Limited-Time Events

Throughout *Monster Hunter Wilds*, there are several events, challenges, and time-limited quests that provide exclusive trading opportunities. These special events often reward players with rare items or materials that are difficult to obtain in the standard gameplay loop. If you're looking to acquire powerful gear quickly or gain an advantage in hunts, these limited-time trading opportunities should not be overlooked.

- **Event Quests with Special Rewards:** Participating in event quests is one of the best ways to acquire exclusive items. These quests often offer rare monster parts, special materials, or unique weapons that can't be obtained through regular gameplay. Completing these quests may require more effort, but the rewards are often worth the investment.

- **Exclusive Vendor Trades During Events:** Keep an eye on event-specific vendors who offer rare items for limited-time exchanges. These merchants might offer items that will drastically improve your combat effectiveness or provide you with a unique visual upgrade for your character. If you want to get your hands on rare items, participating in these special events is a must.

- **Seizing Limited-Time Opportunities:** Some of the best deals in the game come during special seasonal events or time-limited promotions. Be sure to check in during these events for a chance to purchase exclusive gear or acquire rare materials for crafting. These limited-time opportunities are not to be missed if you want to stay ahead of your competition.

8.3 EFFICIENT FARMING FOR MATERIALS AND RESOURCES

In *Monster Hunter Wilds*, acquiring the right materials and resources is crucial to advancing your hunter's journey. From crafting powerful weapons to upgrading armor sets, your success heavily relies on gathering the necessary materials. However, the process can be time-consuming and tedious without a solid farming strategy. In this section, we will explore the most efficient methods to farm materials and resources in the game, ensuring you make the most out of every hunt and exploration.

1. Identifying Key Resource Nodes and Farming Locations

Certain areas in *Monster Hunter Wilds* are rich with specific materials, making them prime farming locations. Knowing where to go and which resources are abundant in these areas will significantly cut down your farming time and help you gather the materials you need more effectively.

- **Best Resource Nodes for Key Materials:** Some of the most valuable materials, such as ores, monster parts, and crafting materials, are found in specific resource nodes scattered throughout the world. Look for these nodes during your hunts or exploration, as they often yield high-quality items that can't be found elsewhere. Areas like caves, cliffs, or dense forests tend to have these resource-rich zones.

- **Understanding the Respawn Mechanics:** Resource nodes and materials in *Monster Hunter Wilds* respawn after a certain amount of time, so it's essential to track these locations and plan your farming trips around them. Once you identify a resource-rich area, you can revisit it regularly to gather more materials without wasting time on long hunts or searches.

- **Farming Monster Parts:** Many key materials come from defeating monsters, but certain monsters drop specific parts that are rarer or harder to obtain. By repeatedly hunting the same monsters in targeted regions, you can maximize your chances of getting these specific materials. Familiarize yourself with monster drop rates and areas where these creatures are found to farm more efficiently.

2. Optimal Farming Routes for Materials

Instead of randomly hunting or exploring, it's far more effective to design specific farming routes that maximize the materials you collect in one go. These routes should connect areas where valuable materials are abundant, minimizing the time it takes to gather everything you need.

- **Mapping Out Efficient Routes:** Before heading out on a farming run, plan your route by identifying regions with abundant resources. Consider how long it will take to travel between each resource node and whether the time invested yields a good return in materials. Efficient routes should not only focus on raw material gathering but also on hunting specific monsters that drop the rarest items.

- **Multi-Resource Areas:** Look for areas that offer multiple types of resources in a single location. For instance, regions that feature both plant-based gathering and monster hunts allow you to diversify your farming, ensuring you're collecting more materials during a single trip. By targeting these areas, you'll make your farming sessions far more productive.

- **Utilizing the Environment:** Pay attention to the environment during your farming runs. Some materials can only be gathered during certain times of the day or weather conditions. If a region has a higher chance of yielding a rare resource under certain conditions (such as rainfall or nightfall), adjust your farming schedule to match these opportunities.

3. Maximizing Farming Efficiency with Boosts and Consumables

To speed up the farming process, you can leverage specific in-game boosts and consumables that increase the number of materials you gather or improve the efficiency of your farming efforts.

- **Using Resource-Boosting Items:** Some items, such as "Lucky Tickets" or specific potions, can boost the number of resources you collect from a single node or monster. These consumables should be used wisely to get the most out of every hunt or exploration run. It's often a good idea to carry a few of these items with you during your farming runs.

- **Boosting Drop Rates:** Certain armor sets or talismans in *Monster Hunter Wilds* are designed to improve the drop rates of materials or increase the chances of obtaining rarer items from monsters. Equip these items during farming runs to significantly boost your chances of collecting high-quality materials.

- **Farming with Friends for Enhanced Drops:** If you're playing in multiplayer mode, joining forces with other hunters can increase the drop rates of rare materials. Co-op farming can be especially useful for hunting high-level monsters or farming large resource nodes. By coordinating your efforts, you can gather materials much faster than you would alone.

4. Reusing and Recycling Materials

Efficient farming isn't just about gathering the right materials it's also about making the most of what you've already collected. Often, you'll have a surplus of materials, some of which may seem useless at first glance. However, knowing how to repurpose and recycle these materials can save you time and resources in the long run.

- **Repurposing Monster Parts and Materials:** Many items you gather, such as monster parts, can be repurposed for crafting or upgrading other pieces of gear. For example, monster bones, claws, and hides can be used to craft armor and weapons, so it's wise to keep track of your inventory and see what can be repurposed for future upgrades.

- **Recycling Materials into Useful Items:** In *Monster Hunter Wilds*, some materials that you don't immediately need can be recycled into other useful resources. For example, spare ore or low-level monster parts can be exchanged for crafting materials that are harder to come by. Keep a lookout for opportunities to recycle surplus materials into higher-tier components.

- **Managing Material Overflow:** As you accumulate large quantities of basic materials, like herbs, ores, or small monster parts, consider selling off the excess to clear up inventory space and earn some extra Zenny. While these materials may not seem valuable individually, they add up over time, providing a consistent income source.

8.4 MANAGING INVENTORY AND CRAFTING RESOURCES WISELY

In *Monster Hunter Wilds*, efficient inventory management and resource allocation are just as important as hunting monsters and crafting gear. The game offers a vast array of materials, weapons, armor, and crafting items, all of which can quickly overwhelm your inventory if not carefully managed. In this section, we'll explore effective ways to manage your resources, prioritize what you collect, and ensure your inventory is always ready for the next big hunt.

1. Organizing Your Inventory for Maximum Efficiency

Keeping your inventory organized is key to preventing clutter and ensuring you can quickly find the materials, weapons, and consumables you need. This not only saves time during hunts but also prevents you from running into resource shortages when you least expect it.

- **Categorize Materials:** Most players find it useful to group similar materials together. For example, keep ores, herbs, and monster parts in separate categories, making it easy to identify what you have in abundance and what you might need to gather more of. By grouping materials logically, you can streamline your crafting and upgrading processes.

- **Use Custom Sort Options:** Many players overlook the inventory sorting options available in the game. Take advantage of the ability to sort your inventory by type, rarity, or value. This will help you quickly identify important materials, while keeping the less useful items out of the way.

- **Keep Essentials Easily Accessible:** Certain consumables, such as healing items, buffs, and traps, are essential for most hunts. Keeping these items easily accessible at the front of your inventory will save you time during combat, allowing you to access the necessary tools without fumbling through your bags in the heat of battle.

2. Prioritizing Crafting Materials and Upgrades

When it comes to crafting and upgrading in *Monster Hunter Wilds*, prioritizing which materials to gather and upgrade is crucial for staying on top of your progression. With limited resources and time, you need to focus on the items that will provide the most benefit in the long run.

- **Identify Key Crafting Materials:** Some materials are more useful than others when it comes to crafting high-tier weapons and armor. For example, monster parts from powerful beasts often play a significant role in crafting legendary gear. Prioritize collecting these specific materials and use them for the best possible upgrades to ensure your hunter is always well-equipped.

- **Track Crafting Recipes:** In *Monster Hunter Wilds*, crafting recipes can be obtained through exploration, quests, or by unlocking new areas. Keeping track of what you can craft will help you focus on gathering the necessary materials. Prioritize unlocking recipes that will provide significant improvements to your gear and abilities, making your hunter stronger for tougher challenges.

- **Crafting vs. Selling:** Sometimes, you'll need to decide whether to craft an item or sell the materials for Zenny. When deciding whether to craft or sell, evaluate the material's rarity and the gear upgrades available. If the material is used in a variety of high-level upgrades, it's probably worth holding onto. If you have a surplus of a certain material with limited uses, consider selling it to free up space and earn extra currency.

3. Avoiding Over-Stocking on Low-Value Items

While it's tempting to hoard every material and item you come across, not all resources are equally valuable in the long run. Avoid cluttering your inventory with items that are easily obtainable or have limited use in crafting. This will help you save space for more important resources.

- **Sell or Discard Excess Items:** If you find yourself collecting excess low-value materials such as common herbs, low-grade ores, or monster parts from easily defeated creatures, it's often a good idea to sell them for Zenny or discard them. Keeping your inventory light on such items allows you to focus on gathering more valuable resources for upgrading your gear.

- **Utilize Storage:** Some areas of *Monster Hunter Wilds* offer storage for extra items that you don't want to throw away but don't have space for in your active inventory. Storing excess materials can be a great way to keep your inventory manageable while still ensuring you have a backup supply of certain materials for future crafting needs.

- **Be Mindful of Stack Sizes:** Some materials and items come in stacks, and if you already have a full stack of a material, you may want to reconsider gathering more of it during a hunt. Pay attention to your current inventory and avoid collecting more of a resource you're already fully stocked on unless it's for a specific upgrade or recipe.

4. Using Resources Wisely During Hunts

Efficient resource management isn't just about inventory it's also about using your resources wisely during hunts. In the heat of battle, it's easy to waste materials on unnecessary buffs or overuse healing items. By being more mindful of how and when to use your resources, you'll save more for future hunts.

- **Plan Your Hunt Loadout:** Before heading out on a hunt, carefully consider your gear and inventory. Equip only the items that will be useful for the specific challenge ahead. For example, if you're hunting a monster with specific elemental weaknesses, make sure to bring the right elemental ammo or traps. Packing wisely helps reduce the need to carry excess items.

- **Conserve Healing Items:** It's easy to spam healing items or potions during a long hunt, but they can quickly run out, leaving you vulnerable later in the battle. Try to conserve healing items by using them only when necessary and by managing your health carefully. Utilize environmental healing sources when available, such as plants or mushrooms found in the field.

- **Trap and Bomb Resources:** Certain traps and bombs are critical for capturing monsters or dealing massive damage. While they can be highly effective, they are also limited in number. Use these resources strategically especially for larger or more difficult monsters ensuring you have them available when the moment counts.

CHAPTER 9: POST-GAME CONTENT AND ENDGAME STRATEGIES

9.1 WHAT TO DO AFTER THE CREDITS ROLL

After completing the main storyline of *Monster Hunter Wilds*, many players find themselves wondering what's next. While defeating the final boss is a massive achievement, the real depth of the game lies in the post-game content. In this chapter, we'll explore the activities, challenges, and strategies that await you after the credits roll. This is where *Monster Hunter Wilds* truly shines, offering a plethora of new opportunities for progression, exploration, and monster hunting.

1. Explore New Areas and Regions

Upon finishing the main story, new regions and zones often become accessible, opening up a wealth of exciting content for players to dive into. These areas typically feature more challenging environments, including tougher monsters, hidden resources, and opportunities for greater rewards.

- **Unlock Hidden Zones:** As the game progresses, certain areas previously shrouded in mystery become open for exploration. These hidden regions may contain unique monster variants, rare crafting materials, and legendary creatures that you couldn't access during the main story. Exploring these zones will allow you to uncover new opportunities for upgrades and challenges.

- **High-Level Hunts in New Environments:** Some areas will introduce tougher monsters with complex behavior and advanced attack patterns. These beasts often require you to adapt your strategies, utilizing new skills, armor, and weapons to succeed. Hunting in these new environments is a true test of your skills, and completing these hunts can grant you high-tier loot and valuable experience.

- **Unlock Post-Game Missions:** Many games, including *Monster Hunter Wilds*, add post-game missions that expand the lore and challenge of the world. These missions often include hunting elite monsters, completing special challenges, or undertaking massive hunts for rare rewards.

2. Take On Advanced Monster Hunts

In the post-game, monsters become increasingly difficult, requiring new strategies and skills to defeat. These advanced hunts often involve rare or powerful monsters that demand a higher level of preparation, teamwork (if in multiplayer mode), and perseverance.

- **Tougher Monster Variants:** Some of the game's most challenging monsters are introduced after the main story concludes. These advanced variants feature improved abilities, altered attack patterns, and higher health, offering a fierce challenge for even the most experienced hunters. Engaging with these monsters not only helps you refine your combat skills but also rewards you with valuable items and crafting materials.

- **Legendary and Mythical Beasts:** In the post-game, certain legendary monsters become available. These creatures are some of the hardest to defeat in the entire game, often requiring specific strategies and maxed-out gear to take down. Hunting them will test your skills and patience, but the rewards such as rare weaponry and powerful armor sets are well worth the effort.

- **Timed Challenges and Events:** Some post-game content includes special event quests that rotate in and out over time. These limited-time events may feature exclusive monsters or special challenges that offer unique rewards not available during the main game. Participating in these quests will help keep the game fresh and provide new challenges to tackle.

3. Maximize Your Hunter's Power

After the story's conclusion, you'll have the opportunity to further develop your hunter through a variety of progression systems. This is where you can truly perfect your build, craft the strongest gear, and push your character to their limits.

- **Level Cap and Skill Enhancements:** While the story may have concluded, the opportunity for character progression doesn't stop there. Post-game, you can level up your hunter's abilities, acquire powerful new skills, and unlock new passive enhancements. This provides a sense of continuous progression, even after the main quest has been completed.

- **Enhance Your Gear to Legendary Status:** Many of the game's best weapons and armor sets are unlocked through post-game challenges or hunts. These sets may require rare materials that can only be obtained after you've completed the main storyline. Maxing out your gear and crafting legendary items will make you even more formidable in battle and ready for the toughest monsters in the game.

- **Perfect Your Monster Hunter Build:** Post-game is the perfect time to fine-tune your hunter's build, experimenting with different weapon loadouts, armor sets, and crafting materials. With more resources at your disposal, you'll have the freedom to optimize your setup for specific hunts, whether you prefer tanking hits, dealing massive damage, or supporting your team.

4. Engage in Endgame Boss Battles

Endgame boss battles are where *Monster Hunter Wilds* truly tests your mettle. These bosses are some of the most difficult and rewarding encounters in the entire game, and they require the best strategies, equipment, and teamwork (if playing in multiplayer).

- **The Final Challenge Bosses:** Some of the game's ultimate challenges are locked behind post-game content, featuring massive beasts or powerful enemies that require all of your experience and skills to defeat. These endgame bosses typically come with unique mechanics, advanced AI, and devastating attacks, making them some of the most thrilling battles in the game.

- **Multistage Fights and Story Expansions:** Certain post-game bosses may not be simple one-off encounters. Some may have multistage fights or multiple phases that test your ability to adapt and plan for changing battle conditions. These multi-layered challenges push your strategic thinking and combat mechanics to the extreme.

- **Epic Rewards for Epic Fights:** Defeating these endgame bosses will often yield some of the best loot in the game, including unique armor, weapons, and crafting materials that can't be found anywhere else. Winning these battles will not only solidify your status as a master hunter but also reward you with the most powerful items in the game.

9.2 UNLOCKING ENDGAME MONSTERS AND HIDDEN BOSSES

Once you've completed the main story in *Monster Hunter Wilds*, the game opens up a whole new level of challenge with the introduction of endgame monsters and hidden bosses. These formidable creatures are designed to test your hunting skills and strategies in ways the standard monsters could not. This section will guide you through the process of unlocking these elusive and powerful monsters, as well as provide tips on how to defeat them.

1. Understanding How Endgame Monsters Are Unlocked

Many of the most challenging monsters in *Monster Hunter Wilds* are hidden behind specific conditions that must be met after the main story is completed. These creatures often feature unique abilities, tougher defenses, and rare loot that make them a worthwhile challenge for seasoned hunters.

- **Progression-Based Unlocks:** After finishing the main game, certain endgame monsters will become available based on your progression. Some may require you to have completed specific quests, while others may only appear once you've hit a certain level or unlocked a particular quest line. Pay attention to any special notifications or NPCs that may hint at their location.

- **Event-Based Unlocks:** Some of the most powerful endgame monsters are tied to special time-limited events that appear after the main game. These monsters are often not available at all times but are rotated in and out of the game through updates or seasonal events. Keep an eye on event schedules and be ready to hunt these creatures while they're active.

- **Rare Monster Encounters:** There are also monsters in *Monster Hunter Wilds* that only appear in very specific environmental conditions, such as during certain weather events or in particular zones that open up after you've reached a specific milestone in the game. Exploring the open world after the main quest can reveal these rare monsters, which often drop exclusive materials.

2. Finding Hidden Bosses in the Wilds

Hidden bosses are another layer of difficulty that await dedicated hunters in the post-game. These bosses often appear in secluded or difficult-to-reach locations and require keen observation and a lot of patience to find.

- **Secret Locations:** Some of the hidden bosses are tied to secret areas within the game world. These areas can be difficult to locate, as they often require solving puzzles or finding obscure pathways. After the main game, explore areas you might have missed, and keep an eye out for strange environmental cues or hidden entrances that could lead you to these hidden bosses.

- **Special Key Items:** Certain endgame bosses are locked behind specific items, such as keys, rare relics, or special tokens that you need to collect throughout your exploration. These items may be found by defeating specific monsters, completing certain side quests, or uncovering hidden secrets in the game world.

- **NPCs and Lore Hints:** NPCs and in-game lore often hold clues about hidden bosses. Some characters may offer cryptic hints, or certain books and journal entries found throughout the world could reveal the locations of these elusive beasts. Be sure to pay attention to everything around you and talk to NPCs as you explore.

3. Strategies for Defeating Endgame Monsters

Endgame monsters in *Monster Hunter Wilds* are designed to push your combat skills to their limits. These creatures feature high-level AI, advanced attack patterns, and massive health pools that can challenge even the most experienced hunters. The following strategies will help you defeat these monsters and earn the incredible rewards they drop.

- **Study Their Attack Patterns:** Endgame monsters often have complex and unpredictable attack patterns. Before engaging in battle, take time to observe their behavior from a safe distance. Learn the timing of their attacks, identify any weaknesses in their patterns, and plan your strategy accordingly.

- **Use Specialized Gear and Weapons:** For each endgame monster, there is usually a weapon or armor set that can give you an edge in battle. These monsters may have specific elemental weaknesses or resistances, so equip yourself with weapons that exploit their vulnerabilities. Be sure to upgrade your gear and select the most suitable armor sets to match your combat style.

- **Take Advantage of the Environment:** Many endgame monsters have massive hitboxes, which makes it difficult to avoid their attacks. However, you can use the environment to your advantage by leading them into traps, environmental hazards, or narrow spaces where their movement is restricted. This strategy is especially effective when fighting hidden bosses in more confined spaces.

- **Multiplayer Cooperation:** Some of the most challenging endgame monsters require teamwork to defeat. If you're tackling a particularly tough boss, consider teaming up with friends or other players in co-op mode. Communication and coordination are key to surviving these intense encounters. Make sure to assign roles, such as tanking, damage dealing, and support, to ensure a balanced approach to the fight.

4. Rare Rewards and Unlockables

Defeating these endgame monsters and hidden bosses is not just about the challenge it's also about the incredible rewards you earn. These monsters drop unique materials, rare weapons, and exclusive armor sets that can significantly enhance your character's strength.

- **Monster-Specific Materials:** Each endgame monster has a set of unique materials that can be used to craft specialized weapons and armor. These materials may be required to upgrade your existing gear or create entirely new equipment that is much stronger than what you've had before. Some rare materials can only be obtained from specific bosses, so hunting them down is worth the effort.

- **Specialized Weapon and Armor Sets:** The most difficult endgame monsters drop some of the game's best loot, including legendary weapon designs and high-end armor sets. These sets are not only stronger than your standard gear but also come with unique attributes and bonuses that can enhance your hunter's performance in specific situations.

- **Achievement and Title Unlocks:** Some players are driven by the need to earn every possible achievement and title. Defeating hidden bosses and unlocking endgame monsters often rewards you with rare trophies or titles that show off your accomplishments. These cosmetic unlocks are purely for bragging rights, but they serve as a badge of honor for completing some of the game's most difficult challenges.

9.3 ULTIMATE CHALLENGES, RAIDS, AND RARE GEAR

As a *Monster Hunter Wilds* veteran, you'll eventually reach the pinnacle of the game's challenges: Ultimate Challenges and Raids. These intense, multi-phase hunts not only push your skills to the limit but also offer some of the best rewards in the game. Rare gear, exclusive materials, and other prestigious items await hunters who are brave enough to take on these ultimate trials. This section will delve into what you need to know about participating in Ultimate Challenges and Raids, and how to secure the rarest gear available.

1. What Are Ultimate Challenges and Raids?

Ultimate Challenges and Raids are some of the most difficult and rewarding content that *Monster Hunter Wilds* has to offer. These are long, multi-stage quests that often require you to face multiple monsters in a single quest or battle through increasingly difficult phases to defeat a series of bosses.

- **Ultimate Challenges:** These are the toughest single encounters that require strategic preparation, perfect execution, and top-tier gear. Ultimate Challenges typically involve facing powerful monsters that have increased health, more aggressive attacks, and additional tricks up their sleeves compared to regular bosses. Some Ultimate Challenges can be triggered after defeating specific endgame monsters or after completing a series of hard quests.

- **Raids:** Raids are cooperative, large-scale events where you team up with other players to defeat a series of powerful monsters in succession. Raids may include multiple waves of enemies, and you'll need to work with your teammates to strategize and defeat each phase. These challenges can take hours to complete and require a high level of coordination and teamwork. While difficult, the rewards from Raids are often unparalleled, offering rare crafting materials, exclusive weapons, and high-end armor sets.

2. How to Prepare for Ultimate Challenges and Raids

Successfully completing Ultimate Challenges and Raids requires more than just basic combat skills it requires thorough preparation and the right approach. Here's how you can prepare for these difficult encounters:

- **Assemble the Right Gear:** Equip yourself with the best weapons and armor available. You'll want to ensure that your gear is upgraded to the highest level possible. Focus on gear that offers resistance to the types of damage or elemental attacks the monsters in these challenges are known for. Pay close attention to the specific weaknesses of the monsters involved and adjust your loadout accordingly.

- **Focus on Stat Buffs and Debuffs:** Ultimate Challenges and Raids often require you to manage status effects like poison, paralysis, and fatigue. Make sure you have gear and items that will either boost your resistances or allow you to cure these debuffs during the hunt. Potions, antidotes, and elemental resistance items are essential for surviving these trials.

- **Strategize with Your Team:** For Raids, communication is key. It's not just about dealing damage team roles should be clearly defined. Assign responsibilities like healing, damage-dealing, and crowd control to make sure the team is well-rounded. Having a hunter that specializes in support or status infliction can make a huge difference. If you're tackling an Ultimate Challenge solo, you'll need to develop a solo strategy that maximizes your efficiency in combat, whether that's focusing on quick dodges or utilizing environmental traps to your advantage.

- **Know the Enemy:** Ultimate Challenges and Raids often feature monsters that are much tougher than any you've faced before. Study their attack patterns, weaknesses, and behaviors before heading into battle. Understanding the monster's attack timings, phases, and weaknesses can give you an edge. Some monsters even have hidden attacks or abilities that may not be obvious at first, so a bit of research and preparation goes a long way.

3. Rare Gear and Exclusive Rewards

Completing Ultimate Challenges and Raids can reward you with some of the most coveted items in *Monster Hunter Wilds*. Here's a breakdown of the rewards you can expect to earn:

- **Legendary Weapons and Armor:** Ultimate Challenges and Raids drop high-quality gear that can't be obtained anywhere else. These include legendary weapons with high attack stats and special abilities, as well as exclusive armor sets that grant unique buffs or resistances. These items often have unique aesthetics that set them apart from the standard gear, making them a mark of prestige for any hunter.

- **Rare Materials for Crafting:** In addition to weapons and armor, the rarest crafting materials are often locked behind these advanced hunts. These materials can be used to upgrade existing gear, create custom armor sets, or craft specialized ammunition or traps. These items are highly valuable and can only be obtained through completion of the most challenging encounters.

- **Exclusive Cosmetics and Titles:** For the truly dedicated hunters, Ultimate Challenges and Raids offer cosmetic rewards such as special hunter outfits, weapon skins, and titles that show off your accomplishments. These cosmetic items are often highly sought after, allowing you to customize your appearance in ways that signal to other players just how accomplished you are in the game.

- **Unique Pets and Companions:** Completing Raids and some Ultimate Challenges also grants you access to exclusive companions or pets that assist you in battle. These companions often have unique abilities and traits, making them useful allies for future hunts. Some pets are more powerful than others, with certain ones offering buffs or healing during combat.

4. Tips for Maximizing Success in Ultimate Challenges and Raids

Participating in these high-stakes hunts requires skill, coordination, and a bit of luck. To help ensure that you come out on top, here are a few additional tips to keep in mind:

- **Use Buffing Items:** During Ultimate Challenges and Raids, the monsters you face can deal massive amounts of damage. Make sure to bring items that buff your stats such as attack boosters, defense enhancers, or items that increase your stamina and health regeneration. These buffs can give you the edge you need in tough battles.

- **Stay Mobile and Alert:** Raids, in particular, are fast-paced and require constant movement. Stay on your toes and be ready to dodge or reposition at a moment's notice. Your survival depends on your ability to react quickly, especially when multiple monsters are involved.

- **Don't Rush:** Ultimate Challenges and Raids are not about speed; they are about strategy and persistence. Rushing through the quest can lead to mistakes or unnecessary deaths. Take your time, coordinate with your teammates, and make sure you are fully prepared before engaging in combat. Patiently whittling down the health of bosses, carefully timing your attacks, and avoiding unnecessary risks will ensure a higher chance of success.

- **Don't Underestimate the Endgame Monsters:** Even if you have completed the base game, be aware that the monsters in Ultimate Challenges and Raids are a whole new level of difficulty. Never underestimate their power. Expect the unexpected, and make sure to bring along all the resources, items, and backup you need.

9.4 REPLAYABILITY TIPS: HOW TO KEEP THE HUNT ALIVE

Once you've reached the endgame of *Monster Hunter Wilds*, you might wonder: how do you keep the hunt alive? After completing major quests and unlocking rare gear, the allure of the game doesn't have to fade. The replayability factor in *Monster Hunter Wilds* is rich, providing countless opportunities to revisit and refine your strategies. Whether you're hunting for more rare materials, experimenting with new playstyles, or challenging yourself in different ways, this section will offer tips to keep your adventures fresh and exciting.

1. Try New Weapon Builds and Playstyles

One of the most enjoyable aspects of *Monster Hunter Wilds* is its variety of weapons, each offering a unique playstyle. After mastering one weapon, consider branching out and trying different builds. Each weapon has its own set of combos, skills, and strategies that can dramatically change your approach to combat.

- **Experiment with Different Weapons:** If you've already used a greatsword or bowgun to hunt your way through the game, try something new like a charge blade or insect glaive. Each weapon type offers a different rhythm and combat experience, allowing you to see the monsters from a new perspective.

- **Focus on Playstyle Variations:** For example, if you're used to a defensive playstyle, try switching to an aggressive damage dealer build or a support role. These shifts can give the game a completely new feel, making every hunt feel like a fresh challenge.

- **Refine Your Skills:** As you gain more experience with a weapon, you can fine-tune your abilities. Keep practicing until you perfect your weapon skills and combos, mastering the nuances of combat for each weapon type.

2. Challenge Yourself with New Difficulty Settings

Once you've conquered the main game, *Monster Hunter Wilds* offers you the opportunity to test your limits through tougher difficulty settings. These enhanced versions of quests ramp up the challenge, pushing your tactical thinking, hunting techniques, and skill to the extreme.

- **Higher Difficulty Quests:** After completing the main game, return to major story missions and side quests with higher difficulty levels enabled. The monsters will be tougher, more resilient, and their attacks even deadlier. Not only does this make for thrilling hunts, but it also rewards you with rarer materials and greater recognition.

- **Solo Hunts:** If you've primarily tackled monsters with a team, consider challenging yourself to go solo. This not only increases the difficulty but also refines your individual combat skills, forcing you to adapt on the fly without the help of teammates.

- **Special Conditions Hunts:** Some quests may feature added challenges like restrictions on equipment or buffs for the monsters. These quests offer unique rewards and keep you on your toes, forcing you to adapt your approach to the hunt.

3. Participate in Seasonal Events and Limited-Time Challenges

Monster Hunter Wilds often features seasonal events, limited-time challenges, and collaborations with other franchises. These events introduce new monsters, rare rewards, and unique tasks that can reignite the excitement of the hunt.

- **Time-Limited Monsters:** Keep an eye on time-limited hunts featuring seasonal or exclusive monsters. These events typically feature harder-to-find monsters with unique mechanics or special rewards that can't be obtained elsewhere.

- **Special Collaborative Content:** Occasionally, the game collaborates with other franchises to introduce special content, such as themed monsters or gear. Engaging with these limited-time quests can bring new experiences and fun into your gameplay.

- **New Cosmetics and Titles:** Events usually come with exclusive cosmetics, titles, and gear, allowing you to customize your hunter's look in new ways. These special rewards help keep the game fresh and motivate you to participate in these time-sensitive challenges.

4. Set Personal Goals and Achievements

If you're looking to keep your motivation high, setting personal goals can be a fantastic way to extend the life of the game. Instead of relying on official content updates or quests, create your own challenges within the game's systems.

- **Master Every Monster:** Aim to hunt and master every monster in the game, including all of the rare and difficult ones. Try completing hunts without using specific tools, like traps or potions, to make the challenge even more difficult.

- **100% Completion:** Strive to complete all side quests, gather every collectible, and craft every piece of gear. This personal challenge can keep you hooked for hundreds of hours as you chase every last item or achievement.

- **Speedrun Challenges:** If you've honed your skills over the course of the game, set goals to complete specific quests or hunts in record time. Racing against the clock adds an entirely new level of excitement, testing your combat efficiency and knowledge of each monster's weaknesses.

5. Engage with the Community and Share Your Progress

One of the most enjoyable aspects of *Monster Hunter Wilds* is its passionate community of hunters. Engaging with other players, whether through online forums or social media, can breathe new life into your gameplay experience.

- **Share Your Hunts and Builds:** Showcase your weapon loadouts, armor sets, and hunting strategies with other players. You may pick up new ideas for playstyles or discover new builds that you hadn't considered.

- **Join Online Competitions:** Participate in online hunting events or leaderboards to compete with others for the fastest, most efficient hunts. Whether it's a solo challenge or a team-based competition, competing with others adds a competitive element to the game and can reignite your passion for the hunt.

- **Engage in Community Challenges:** Many gaming communities host challenges such as "no damage" runs, unique weapon-only hunts, or community goals that bring players together to work toward a common objective. These events can be both fun and rewarding as you interact with other players and take part in something larger than just your own progress.

CHAPTER 10: ACHIEVEMENTS AND TROPHY GUIDE

10.1 COMPLETE TROPHY AND ACHIEVEMENT LIST

Monster Hunter Wilds is a game filled with rewarding experiences, and achieving the coveted trophies and achievements is one of the most satisfying aspects of the game. As you hunt, explore, and conquer the vast wilds, you'll be rewarded with achievements that reflect your skill and dedication. This section provides a complete list of all trophies and achievements available, categorizing them by difficulty and offering you a clear roadmap to collect them all.

Note: Each trophy has its own set of conditions that you must meet to unlock it. Some are fairly easy to obtain, while others require persistence, strategy, and considerable expertise. As a hunter, you'll need to overcome various challenges to complete the entire list, but with the right guidance, it's entirely possible to unlock them all.

1. Bronze Trophies: The Foundation of the Hunt

The bronze trophies are a testament to your early progress and learning in *Monster Hunter Wilds*. These are the simplest achievements, generally unlocked as you familiarize yourself with the game's mechanics, characters, and environments.

- **Beginner Hunter:** Complete your first hunt.
- **First Strike:** Successfully land a hit on a monster.
- **Master of the Basics:** Complete a basic tutorial quest.
- **Resourceful Gatherer:** Collect 100 different materials.
- **Weapon Prodigy:** Craft your first weapon.

While these are often earned during your initial gameplay, they serve as the foundation for your future accomplishments. Unlocking them early on will provide a sense of progression and encourage you to push forward into more challenging content.

2. Silver Trophies: Advancing the Hunt

Silver trophies are awarded for more difficult feats, requiring you to master gameplay mechanics, strategize carefully, and develop your skills as a hunter. Earning these trophies signals a deeper understanding of *Monster Hunter Wilds*.

- **Monster Slayer:** Defeat 50 unique monsters.
- **Weapon Master:** Fully upgrade one weapon to its maximum tier.
- **True Explorer:** Discover every major area in the game.
- **Perfect Preparation:** Complete a quest using only crafted materials (no items purchased).
- **Teamwork Victory:** Complete a co-op quest with four players.

These trophies are designed to push you beyond the basics, encouraging you to venture into tougher content, make tactical decisions, and explore every corner of the game. They showcase your increasing expertise and commitment to the hunt.

3. Gold Trophies: Elite Hunter Status

Gold trophies are the pinnacle of achievements in *Monster Hunter Wilds*. Earning these is a true mark of mastery, requiring deep strategy, precise combat skills, and immense dedication. Gold trophies are often unlocked after completing significant milestones or defeating the most difficult of monsters.

- **Endgame Conqueror:** Complete the game's hardest difficulty level.
- **Legendary Hunter:** Defeat all high-ranking monsters and complete all major quests.
- **Flawless Victory:** Defeat a monster without taking any damage in a single fight.
- **Resource Hoarder:** Gather over 10,000 materials across all hunts.
- **Master of Crafting:** Create every single item, weapon, and piece of armor in the game.

Earning gold trophies requires hours of dedicated hunting and strategic planning. These rewards are for those who are truly invested in *Monster*

Hunter Wilds, consistently testing their skills and pushing the limits of what is possible.

4. Platinum Trophy: The Ultimate Achievement

The platinum trophy is the crowning achievement for any true *Monster Hunter Wilds* player. This is only unlocked once you've earned every other trophy in the game. It signifies the completion of all challenges, quests, and accomplishments that the game has to offer. This is the trophy that symbolizes your journey from a novice to a legendary hunter.

- **Wilds Master:** Unlock all trophies and complete every challenge in the game.

To earn the platinum trophy, you will need to dedicate yourself to mastering every aspect of the game. From understanding the deepest mechanics of combat to completing every quest, monster hunt, and side mission, the platinum trophy is reserved for the ultimate completionist.

Tips for Earning Trophies Efficiently

While achieving every trophy in *Monster Hunter Wilds* is a significant accomplishment, it can also be a lengthy journey. Here are a few tips to make your pursuit of trophies more efficient and enjoyable:

1. Plan Your Progression

- **Start with Bronze Trophies:** As you complete basic quests and get familiar with the mechanics, the bronze trophies will come naturally. Focus on these first to build your confidence.
- **Move on to Silver Trophies:** Once you've grasped the game's fundamentals, set your sights on silver trophies. These achievements will require more time, but they're still manageable and reward steady progress.
- **Tackle Gold Trophies After Mastering Mechanics:** Gold trophies require considerable effort. Start focusing on high-level gameplay and engage in challenging hunts to unlock these prestigious awards.

2. Use Co-op Hunts to Your Advantage

Co-op hunts can be a massive help, especially for tougher monsters and specific trophies. Not only do they make the hunts more manageable, but they also help unlock co-op-related trophies. Plus, playing with friends adds another layer of fun to the process.

3. Don't Forget About Side Quests

Many side quests and event quests reward you with special trophies. These can sometimes be overlooked, but they're an excellent way to rack up achievements while diversifying your hunting experience.

4. Maximize Resource Gathering and Crafting

Many of the trophies related to crafting and material collection can be achieved through steady resource farming. While this may seem like a grind, it's an excellent way to improve your overall skill set while earning silver and gold trophies.

10.2 HARDEST ACHIEVEMENTS AND HOW TO UNLOCK THEM

Some of the most difficult achievements in *Monster Hunter Wilds* require precision, time, and an immense amount of strategy. These challenges will test your abilities and perseverance, pushing you to be the best hunter you can be. In this section, we will break down the hardest trophies and provide step-by-step advice on how to unlock them.

1. Flawless Victory: Defeat a Monster Without Taking Any Damage

Description: This achievement is among the hardest in the game. To unlock it, you must defeat a monster in combat without taking any damage, no matter how skilled you are. This means dodging every single attack and being perfect in your timing and positioning.

How to Unlock:

- **Choose the Right Monster:** This achievement is easier when you focus on lower-tier monsters with more predictable attacks. Start with a monster you are comfortable with and that you know well.
- **Master Dodging and Parrying:** The key to success is flawless dodging and parrying. Practice these techniques until you can

execute them without fail. Make sure you have the correct armor and skills equipped to boost your agility.

- **Utilize Environmental Hazards:** Some monsters can be stunned or knocked down using environmental hazards. Learn where these are in each area to make the fight easier. This gives you a chance to heal or reposition without taking damage.
- **Patience is Key:** This achievement might require multiple attempts. Take your time, learn the monster's attack patterns, and adjust your strategy as needed. Don't rush getting hit even once will fail the achievement.

2. Legendary Hunter: Defeat All High-Ranking Monsters and Complete All Major Quests

Description: To unlock this achievement, you must defeat all the high-ranking monsters in *Monster Hunter Wilds* and complete every major quest. High-ranking monsters are some of the toughest opponents, and you'll need to be at the top of your game to beat them.

How to Unlock:

- **Reach High Rank:** Ensure you have completed all lower-tier hunts and are sufficiently advanced in your story. High-ranking monsters are unlocked after you progress through the main story.
- **Focus on Gear Upgrades:** Before taking on high-ranking monsters, make sure your gear is at its best. Upgrade your weapons and armor, craft the highest tier of healing and boosting items, and ensure you're well-prepared.
- **Master Combat Mechanics:** High-ranking monsters come with a higher difficulty, and their attack patterns are more complex. Make sure you've fully mastered your weapon and understand how to dodge, block, and counter effectively.
- **Be Strategic in Co-op Hunts:** For the toughest monsters, playing in a co-op team is often the best strategy. Working with others will help you cover more ground, and you'll be able to stagger the monster's attacks to make the hunt more manageable.

3. Master of Crafting: Create Every Weapon and Piece of Armor in the Game

Description: This achievement challenges your crafting skills by requiring you to create every single weapon, armor set, and accessory available. The process can be long, but the reward is significant as you unlock the full potential of crafting in *Monster Hunter Wilds*.

How to Unlock:

- **Complete Major Hunts for Materials:** Crafting materials can be rare, especially for high-end armor and weapons. Focus on hunting specific monsters that drop valuable crafting components. Some of the rarer materials come from high-ranking or special event monsters.
- **Invest Time in Resource Farming:** Gathering materials will require farming specific areas or repeating certain quests. Look for areas with abundant resources and keep track of the resources you need to complete your full set.
- **Upgrade Your Equipment Regularly:** Ensure your armor and weapons are upgraded as you progress. While crafting every single item is a lengthy process, it will eventually pay off as you collect the materials required for more advanced pieces.

4. Monster Slayer: Defeat 500 Unique Monsters

Description: This achievement is a marathon rather than a sprint. Defeating 500 unique monsters requires a lot of time and effort, but each victory will bring you one step closer to unlocking this coveted achievement.

How to Unlock:

- **Set a Farming Routine:** Start by focusing on the early and mid-tier monsters that appear frequently in the game. These monsters offer the best opportunities for quick hunts and will help you rack up kills without spending too much time.
- **Participate in Event Hunts:** Event hunts and special quests often feature rare monsters. These hunts not only help you diversify your monster-killing experience but also give you a chance to earn additional rewards and progress faster toward this achievement.
- **Play Co-op Hunts:** In co-op hunts, monsters are often easier to defeat, especially with a well-coordinated team. Use these opportunities to take down more monsters in less time, and be sure to keep track of all the unique ones you've defeated.

5. Endgame Conqueror: Complete the Game's Hardest Difficulty Level

Description: The "Endgame Conqueror" trophy requires you to complete the game on its hardest difficulty setting. Monsters are more aggressive, environmental hazards are deadlier, and every mistake you make can cost you the entire hunt. Only the most experienced and well-prepared hunters can achieve this.

How to Unlock:

- **Fully Upgrade Your Gear:** The hardest difficulty requires the best possible gear. Ensure you have the highest-tier weapons, armor, and healing items before venturing into these hunts. Having access to top-level gear will be essential for survival.
- **Know Your Monsters:** In the hardest difficulty, monsters hit harder and have more advanced attack patterns. Spend time learning the mechanics and weaknesses of each high-level monster to anticipate their moves and avoid unnecessary damage.
- **Form a Co-op Group:** Even with the best equipment, it's unlikely you'll succeed in the hardest difficulty without a strong team. Form a co-op group with reliable teammates who complement your playstyle and help cover each other during tough fights.
- **Complete All Side Quests First:** Before jumping into the hardest difficulty, make sure you've completed all side quests and earned extra rewards, materials, and upgrades. This will give you an edge in your final, endgame hunts.

Tips for Unlocking the Hardest Achievements:

- **Consistency Is Key:** Many of the hardest achievements, like defeating 500 unique monsters, require grinding. Stay consistent with your hunts, and don't rush through the game. Patience will ultimately lead to success.
- **Focus on One Achievement at a Time:** Attempting to unlock multiple difficult trophies at once can lead to burnout. Focus on one challenging achievement at a time to avoid frustration and maximize your efforts.
- **Use the Right Equipment:** Don't underestimate the importance of having the best weapons and armor. Prioritize upgrading your gear to match the difficulty of the challenges you are undertaking.
- **Play With Friends:** Co-op play can make some of the toughest achievements easier. Join up with friends or use matchmaking to form strong hunting parties for particularly difficult monsters.

10.3 BEST STRATEGIES FOR 100% COMPLETION

Achieving 100% completion in *Monster Hunter Wilds* is a monumental task that requires more than just defeating monsters. You'll need to focus on every aspect of the game from mastering combat mechanics to completing side quests, crafting, and collecting every item. Here, we'll break down the best strategies to help you achieve that coveted 100% completion and become a true Monster Hunter expert.

1. Prioritize Key Quests and Monster Hunts

Description: Monster Hunter Wilds has a vast number of quests and hunts to tackle, but not all of them are necessary for completion. To reach 100%, you'll need to complete every story quest, side quest, and hunt all the available monsters, including special event monsters.

How to Unlock 100% Completion:

- **Focus on Main and Side Quests:** Completing the main story quests is essential for unlocking new areas and hunting opportunities. However, side quests offer valuable rewards and often help unlock rare materials and special abilities. Prioritize these as you advance through the game, ensuring that you don't skip any.
- **Hunt All Monsters:** Every monster in the game has unique attributes, materials, and rewards. Keep track of the ones you've hunted, and make sure you've defeated them all. Special event monsters and rare hunts are especially rewarding, offering materials needed for crafting and upgrading your gear.
- **Finish Time-Limited Events:** Some of the most elusive achievements can be tied to limited-time events. Check regularly for special hunts, challenges, and collaborations that reward exclusive monsters or gear, making sure not to miss any.

2. Maximize Gear and Crafting

Description: One of the key aspects of 100% completion is crafting and upgrading your weapons, armor, and accessories. The game features a deep crafting system that requires materials dropped by monsters, gathered resources, and special rewards.

How to Unlock 100% Completion:

- **Craft Every Weapon and Armor Set:** Aim to collect and craft all weapon types, armor sets, and accessories. This involves gathering materials from a wide range of monsters and ensuring you farm efficiently for rare materials.
- **Upgrade Everything:** Don't just craft new gear make sure to fully upgrade your weapons and armor. This often requires specific monster drops, so it's vital to track what you need and upgrade your equipment regularly to stay prepared for tougher battles.
- **Learn Crafting Recipes:** Explore every crafting recipe available. Some are unlocked by completing specific quests, while others require rare materials from high-ranking monsters or exploration. Master crafting to create potent potions, bombs, and other useful items.

3. Master Combat and Mechanics

Description: Combat is the core of *Monster Hunter Wilds*. To achieve 100% completion, you'll need to master all aspects of combat, from basic attacks to advanced strategies for handling the most challenging monsters in the game.

How to Unlock 100% Completion:

- **Master Every Weapon:** While focusing on your preferred weapon is essential, to achieve true completion, you should master all weapon types. Each weapon offers a unique playstyle, and understanding their strengths and weaknesses will help you take on different monsters more efficiently.
- **Optimize Combat Strategies:** Learn to use all combat mechanics dodging, parrying, and counterattacks effectively. In addition to mastering basic combat, you'll need to become proficient at using these advanced techniques to take down difficult monsters without taking unnecessary damage.
- **Take on All Difficulty Levels:** Once you've beaten the game, challenge yourself with higher difficulty levels. Completing all quests, monsters, and challenges in the hardest difficulty will contribute to your goal of 100% completion.

4. Explore Every Corner and Collect All Resources

Description: Exploration is vital to your 100% completion journey. Hidden areas, rare materials, and collectibles are scattered throughout the world. You'll need to thoroughly explore every zone to find these secrets.

How to Unlock 100% Completion:

- **Explore Every Map Thoroughly:** Each environment in *Monster Hunter Wilds* has hidden areas, secret passages, and collectible materials. Spend time exploring every corner of the map and interacting with environmental features to uncover hidden resources.
- **Track Rare Collectibles:** Collect every rare item, material, and resource in the game. Some materials may seem difficult to find, but persistent exploration and gathering will ensure that you have everything you need for crafting and upgrading.
- **Maximize Farming:** Farming specific zones for resources like herbs, ores, and monster parts is essential. Use environmental hazards, traps, and the game's dynamic weather to your advantage when farming for hard-to-find materials.

5. Fully Complete the Hunter's Journal

Description: One of the most time-consuming tasks in achieving 100% completion is fully filling out the Hunter's Journal. This journal tracks all the monsters you've encountered, the gear you've crafted, and the activities you've completed. To get 100%, you'll need to ensure every entry is filled.

How to Unlock 100% Completion:

- **Track Monster Encounters:** Make sure you've hunted every unique monster in the game. This includes main story monsters, side quest monsters, rare monsters, and special event monsters. Keep track of your journal and mark off every monster you defeat.
- **Complete All Gear Entries:** As you craft and upgrade your weapons and armor, be sure to register every item in the journal. Each new item will unlock new entries, helping you get closer to completion.
- **Complete All Activities and Achievements:** Your Hunter's Journal also tracks achievements, side quests, and progress. Completing all activities and unlocking all trophies and

achievements will fill out your journal and bring you closer to that coveted 100% completion.

6. Commit to Co-op and Multiplayer

Description: Completing the game's multiplayer content is essential for full completion. Co-op hunts, multiplayer quests, and team-based challenges will all contribute to your progress.

How to Unlock 100% Completion:

- **Join Multiplayer Hunts:** Participate in a variety of multiplayer hunts with friends or random players to earn unique rewards and trophies. These co-op hunts are required to unlock some of the rare monsters, quests, and special items.
- **Coordinate with Friends for Event Quests:** Many of the game's event quests can only be completed in multiplayer mode. Make sure to regularly join events with friends or online communities to maximize your rewards and complete all available content.

7. Time-Limited Content and Special Events

Description: Certain content in *Monster Hunter Wilds* is only available for a limited time, including special event quests and seasonal hunts. To unlock every aspect of the game, you'll need to participate in these events before they disappear.

How to Unlock 100% Completion:

- **Check for Time-Limited Events:** Keep an eye on the game's calendar for special events and collaborations. These events often offer exclusive monsters, rare items, or limited-time challenges that are essential for full completion.
- **Complete Seasonal Hunts:** Many seasonal events feature exclusive monsters and themed challenges. Make sure you participate in these events to collect special gear and achievements before they vanish.

8. Achieve All Trophies and Achievements

Description: One of the final steps to achieving 100% completion is unlocking every trophy and achievement in the game. This requires a combination of skill, time, and persistence, as some trophies are tied to difficult tasks or achievements.

How to Unlock 100% Completion:

- **Complete Hard-to-Get Achievements:** Focus on the hardest achievements, such as defeating certain monsters, reaching specific milestones, or completing challenges. Utilize the strategies outlined in the previous chapter to help you unlock these trophies.
- **Use Strategy Guides:** If you find yourself struggling with a particularly difficult trophy or achievement, refer to online resources or strategy guides for tips and tricks to make the process easier.

10.4 SPEEDRUN TIPS FOR TROPHY HUNTERS

For those looking to complete *Monster Hunter Wilds* in record time while also unlocking trophies, speedrunning can be an exciting and challenging way to achieve both goals. Speedrunning not only tests your efficiency in gameplay but also allows you to experience the game's mechanics in a new light. This section will guide you through essential tips for mastering speedruns, while also giving you the best strategies for earning trophies quickly.

1. Plan Your Route and Focus on Key Objectives

Description: Speedrunning is all about efficiency, and to achieve a fast completion time, you'll need to plan your route strategically. Focus on completing only the key objectives that contribute to progression, while avoiding distractions that can waste precious time.

Speedrun Tips:

- **Prioritize Main Quests:** Skip unnecessary side content in your first run. The primary goal is to get through the main story and unlock essential gear, so stick to the critical quests.
- **Skip Unnecessary Combat:** Only engage with monsters when absolutely necessary for progression. Avoid time-wasting battles unless they reward you with crucial items or experience points.
- **Efficient Farming:** While you want to skip most farming, there are specific points in the game where gathering rare materials or

crafting key items can speed up your overall journey. Plan for the most time-effective farming points.

2. Master the Combat System for Speed and Efficiency

Description: Combat in *Monster Hunter Wilds* is complex, but speedrunning demands efficiency in every fight. You'll need to use combat techniques that minimize time while still achieving victory.

Speedrun Tips:

- **Weapon Choice:** Choose weapons that allow for fast attacks and quick monster takedowns. Weapons like the Sword & Shield or Dual Blades are often preferred for speedrunning due to their speed and maneuverability.
- **Know Monster Weaknesses:** Efficiently target weak points and exploit monster weaknesses. You'll need to understand which monsters are weak to certain elements to finish them faster.
- **Use Power-ups Wisely:** Maximize the use of buffs and healing items, especially in fights against tougher monsters. Have your best healing items equipped for emergency use, but try to avoid excessive item consumption that slows you down.

3. Take Advantage of Shortcuts and Skip Animations

Description: Skipping animations, cutscenes, and loading screens can shave off valuable seconds. Knowing the layout of maps and recognizing shortcut routes can save significant time throughout your playthrough.

Speedrun Tips:

- **Skip Cutscenes and Dialogues:** Always skip cutscenes and dialogues to reduce time spent on non-interactive segments. This includes any story or character interactions, so get into the habit of rapidly pressing buttons to skip.
- **Use Fast Travel and Shortcuts:** Make use of fast travel options to quickly move between locations, and utilize map shortcuts to avoid long traversal paths. Learn the most efficient routes to travel between key areas, especially those involving critical quests or hunts.

- **Avoid Excessive Exploration:** While exploring can be fun, it takes time. Stick to the critical paths unless exploration rewards you with something vital for completing quests or acquiring trophies.

4. Optimize Inventory and Resource Management

Description: Inventory management can slow down your speedrun if you're not careful. Keep your inventory optimized for speed, avoiding time-consuming management during hunts.

Speedrun Tips:

- **Pre-select Items:** Before embarking on hunts or quests, make sure you have the necessary items prepared. Carry only the essentials, such as healing potions, traps, or buffs. This will save time spent in the menus during hunts.
- **Upgrade Gear Efficiently:** Only upgrade essential equipment that will significantly improve your combat abilities. Don't waste time on non-critical upgrades during your speedrun, especially for weapons or armor that you don't plan to use for the duration of the run.
- **Auto-sell Unneeded Items:** If you're collecting items on your way, set your character to auto-sell materials that you won't need, such as low-grade materials or consumables. This reduces the need for frequent inventory checks and management.

5. Master Time-Based Challenges for Speedrun Achievements

Description: Some trophies and achievements require specific actions within a time limit, such as defeating certain monsters within a set timeframe. To complete these challenges, you'll need to focus on both speed and combat efficiency.

Speedrun Tips:

- **Prepare for Timed Hunts:** Some hunts will have time-based objectives, and completing them quickly is key for earning trophies. Focus on preparing your weapons and armor, as well as using buffs that can increase your damage output for these hunts.
- **Perfect Your Timing on Quick Hunts:** Some trophies require the defeat of monsters in as little time as possible. Practice strategies for handling these hunts and make sure to time your attacks

perfectly. Use fast weapons and take advantage of monster stun opportunities for quick kills.

6. Practice, Refine, and Track Your Runs

Description: Like any other speedrun, practice is crucial. Regularly refining your speedrun skills and tracking your progress is essential for improving times and unlocking achievements.

Speedrun Tips:

- **Use Practice Runs:** Set up specific practice sessions focused on improving your speedrun time for certain areas, monsters, or hunts. Try different strategies to figure out the most time-efficient way to clear sections of the game.
- **Track Your Progress:** Utilize speedrun trackers or timers to measure your performance and identify areas where you can shave off seconds. Compare your times with other speedrun records for tips on improving efficiency.

7. Participate in Speedrun Communities

Description: Joining speedrun communities will provide you with valuable insights, strategies, and tips from other seasoned players. These communities are a great place to learn new techniques and share your speedrun results.

Speedrun Tips:

- **Join Forums and Speedrun Groups:** Participate in forums or Discord groups dedicated to *Monster Hunter Wilds* speedrunning. Other players can provide you with tips, tricks, and alternative strategies that you might not have considered.
- **Watch Speedrun Videos:** Watching experienced speedrunners complete the game can be an excellent learning opportunity. Observe their techniques, weapon choices, and routing strategies to gain new insights into improving your own run.

www.ingramcontent.com/pod-product-compliance
Lightning Source LLC
LaVergne TN
LVHW051243050326
832903LV00028B/2556